# Gender and Social Psychology

'Excellent. A comprehensive summary, drawing on a wide range of literature. Her style is clear and enjoyable, her analysis critical and sharp. The student new to this area (whether in their first or final year) will certainly come away informed.'

Suzanne Zeedyk, *University of Dundee*

'Very clear and interesting. . . . Easy to understand, especially for those students with no background in Psychology. The material and examples appeal to the everyday experience of most students.'

Barbara Deguzis, *research student, Bolton Institute*

*Gender and Social Psychology* critically evaluates the contribution that psychology has made to the study of gender, examining key issues such as family roles and parenting, inequalities in education, jobs and pay, and the effects of media representation of the sexes.

Vivien Burr explains theory and research in an accessible and thorough manner, and weaves together psychological, sociological and feminist approaches to provide an understanding of gender which is more complete than that typically offered by psychology texts.

**Vivien Burr** is Senior Lecturer in Psychology at the University of Huddersfield. Her previous publications include *An Introduction to Social Constructionism* (1995).

# Psychology Focus

## Series editor: Perry Hinton, University of Luton

The Psychology Focus series provides students with a new focus on key topic areas in psychology. It supports students taking modules in psychology, whether for a psychology degree or a combined programme, and those renewing their qualification in a related discipline. Each short book:

- presents clear, in-depth coverage of a discrete area with many applied examples
- assumes no prior knowledge of psychology
- has been written by an experienced teacher
- has chapter summaries, annotated further reading and a glossary of key terms.

Also available in this series:

# Gender
# and Social
# Psychology

■ Vivien Burr

LONDON AND NEW YORK

ROUTLEDGE

*British Library Cataloguing in
Publication Data*
A catalogue record for this book is
available from the British Library

*Library of Congress Cataloging in
Publication Data*
Burr, Vivien.
Gender and social psychology / Vivien
Burr
p. cm. – (Psychology focus)
Includes bibliographical references
and index.
1. Sex role. 2. Social psychology.
3. Sex differences.
(Psychology) I. Title. II. Series.
HQ1075.B875 1998
133.3'3–dc21      97–37617

ISBN 0–415–15814–1 (hbk)
ISBN 0–415–15815–X (pbk)

# Contents

# CONTENTS

# Series preface

The Psychology Focus series provides short, up-to-date accounts of key areas in psychology without assuming the reader's prior knowledge in the subject. Psychology is often a favoured subject area for study, since it is relevant to a wide range of disciplines such as Sociology, Education, Nursing and Business Studies. These relatively inexpensive but focused short texts combine sufficient detail for psychology specialists with sufficient clarity for non-specialists.

The series authors are academics experienced in undergraduate teaching as well as research. Each takes a key topic within their area of psychological expertise and presents a short review, highlighting important themes and including both theory and research findings. Each aspect of the topic is clearly explained with supporting glossaries to elucidate technical terms.

The series has been conceived within the context of the increasing modularisation which has been developed in higher education over the last decade

and fulfils the consequent need for clear, focused, topic-based course material. Instead of following one course of study, students on a modularisation programme are often able to choose modules from a wide range of disciplines to complement the modules they are required to study for a specific degree. It can no longer be assumed that students studying a particular module will necessarily have the same background knowledge (or lack of it!) in that subject. But they will need to familiarise themselves with a particular topic rapidly since a single module in a single topic may be only 15 weeks long, with assessments arising during that period. They may have to combine eight or more modules in a single year to obtain a degree at the end of their programme of study.

One possible problem with studying a range of separate modules is that the relevance of a particular topic or the relationship between topics may not always be apparent. In the Psychology Focus series, authors have drawn where possible on practical and applied examples to support the points being made so that readers can see the wider relevance of the topic under study. Also, the study of psychology is usually broken up into separate areas, such as social psychology, developmental psychology and cognitive psychology, to take three examples. Whilst the books in the Psychology Focus series will provide excellent coverage of certain key topics within these 'traditional' areas the authors have not been constrained in their examples and explanations and may draw on material across the whole field of psychology to help explain the topic under study more fully.

Each text in the series provides the reader with a range of important material on a specific topic. They are suitably comprehensive and give a clear account of the important issues involved. The authors analyse and interpret the material as well as present an up-to-date and detailed review of key work. Recent references are provided along with suggested further reading to allow readers to investigate the topic in more depth. It is hoped, therefore, that after following the informative review of a key topic in a Psychology Focus text, readers will not only have a clear understanding of the issues in question but will be intrigued and challenged to investigate the topic further.

# Acknowledgements

My thanks are due in particular to Perry Hinton for his helpful comments and suggestions, which, in their non-judgemental character, exemplified the term 'constructive criticism'. I am indebted also to Phil Salmon for her prompt and thorough feedback on Chapter 3, and for her many kind words of encouragement. Last but not least, thanks again to Geoff Adams for allowing me to prevail upon our friendship yet again for the preparation of the index.

# Key issues and perspectives

1

## Why study gender?

It is often the case that what seem to be the most mundane aspects of our lives, those which we rarely question or even think about, are actually quite crucial aspects of our existence as human beings. We are rarely conscious of the air we breathe, or of the act of breathing. Nevertheless, they are fundamental to our continued existence. In the same way, **gender** is the backcloth against which our daily lives are played out. It suffuses our existence so that, like breathing, it becomes invisible to us because of its familiarity. White says:

> It is enough to make the point to ask: of all the things you might potentially fail to register or remember about someone, when did you ever forget what sex someone was, even after the most fleeting encounter? We remember because, whether we wish it so or not, sex is significant and it is this significance that is called gender.
>
> (White, 1989: 17–18)

When we begin to examine the minutiae of routine daily life, it soon becomes clear that there is virtually no aspect of it which is not gendered. It is commonplace to remark upon and to question what we now think of as obvious differences and inequalities in the way women and men, boys and girls, behave and are treated. We know about the differences in toys that are thought appropriate for male and female children, about the different **roles** that women and men play in the family, and about the gender differences in jobs and careers, although it is only in relatively recent times that these differences have become problematised (that is, they have only relatively recently come to be regarded as problems). However, there are many more subtle ways in which our lives are gendered. Here are some examples which I'm sure you can relate to your own experience:

- Women and men differ in their 'body language'. They carry themselves differently, adopt different postures when seated, and use gestures and expressions differently when talking. In a way, we don't even have to appeal to research evidence to see that this is so – the antics of the drag queen are funny precisely because he is exploiting these differences.

- In conversation, too, there are differences of which we may be quite unaware at a conscious level (see Swann, 1992). In mixed sex groups, men interrupt more and offer more direct requests and statements, whereas women are more likely to be interrupted, to make indirect requests and to give more conversational 'support' to other speakers (by saying 'Mmm', 'Yeah' etc., or by asking questions).

- When we see someone's handwriting for the first time, we intuitively feel that we can tell the sex of the writer from its shape and form. Even if we were completely inaccurate in our judgements (which I don't think we are) it is surely significant that we easily read gender into mundane activities such as writing. (Although I have never seen any research in this area, on the gender course that I teach we begin each year by asking the students to guess whether certain extracts from past students' assessments were penned by a woman or a man, and the results are surprisingly consistent).

- In countless ways, we mark our gender in our choice of personal possessions when, on the face of it, there are no practical reasons for this gendering. The considerable differences in size and/or styling between ladies' and men's wrist-watches, socks, slippers, handkerchiefs, fragrances, jewellery, electric razors and so on cannot be justified solely by physical differences between the sexes. Forty years ago, it would have been a dreadful embarrassment to have one's hair parted on the wrong side of the head, and today men's and women's clothing is still buttoned on opposite sides of the garment.

I earlier used the word 'subtle' rather than 'trivial' to describe the kinds of differences I have illustrated above partly because attempts to problematise gender differences have been resisted with the argument that these differences are trivial. In the examples shown, it may be argued that these subtle gender differences are intimately bound up in the larger, more obvious gender differences that we are used to thinking about as problems, and that they are therefore in no way trivial, especially for the social scientist.

The examples show, at the very least, that much of our routine daily life embodies clear messages about 'difference'. When we distinguish between the sexes in ways which do not necessarily have a functional basis, like when children are made to line up as girls and boys at school or when their names are organised by sex on the register, we are imparting strong messages about difference and separateness. The examples can also tell us something about appropriate **masculinity** and **femininity**. Given the increasing role that personal possessions are playing in providing our sense of identity, the meanings carried by such things as fluffy slippers or Kleenex for Men provide important information about what it currently means to be appropriately masculine or feminine in the western world. There is also something to be learned about gender relations. Women's and men's body language and the pattern of their interactions together are not simply about arbitrary stylistic differences. There are important messages here about how we feel we are able to occupy space (both physical space and linguistic space), and about how conversation between women and men is suffused with power relations.

These things are all implicated in the larger picture, where we can observe the more obvious differences and inequalities between women and men. There is a tendency today to consider the battle for equality largely won, and to say that we now live in a 'post-feminist' society (one where **feminism** is no longer needed). The Equal Pay Act (1970), The **Sex Discrimination** Act (1975) and the setting up of the Equal Opportunities Commission (EOC) are markers of a society which acknowledges its own inequalities and is setting about redressing the balance. Nevertheless, despite these measures it is still the case that women and men in contemporary western societies (which are the focus of this book) do not enjoy equality.

Although women make up nearly 50 per cent of the workforce in Britain, on average their pay is approximately two-thirds that of men, and they are more likely than men to be found in low-paid, part-time and insecure employment. Across the range of work sectors, men are more likely than women to occupy high status, powerful positions (this is referred to as the '**vertical gender division of labour**'). In organisations, the managers are generally men and their assistants and secretarial staff women. Even in occupations dominated by women in terms of sheer numbers, such as teaching and nursing, men who enter these professions stand a better than average chance of reaching the top positions. In terms of the kinds of jobs that people do, it is still the case that there are women's jobs, in the caring and service industries, and men's jobs, in industry and commerce (this is referred to as the '**horizontal gender division of labour**'). In secondary education, the GCSE and A level subjects taken by girls and boys still show a gender bias, with boys favouring the hard sciences and technology, and girls opting for languages and the humanities (with knock-on consequences for choices of well-paid jobs and careers which are then open to them). In the family, despite the fact that women are entering full- or part-time employment outside of the home, they are still primarily responsible for the running of the household and spend considerably more time in childcare and household tasks than men.

In economic terms, then, women still have a good deal of catching up to do. They are less likely than men to have access to well-paid, secure employment and are more likely to be constrained by domestic responsibilities. In terms of access to non-traditional roles, it can be argued that men also get a raw deal. They may find it difficult to obtain employment in traditionally female areas of work, for example as a nursery nurse or childminder, and it is clear that at least some men feel that their lives do not give them enough opportunities to become fully involved in bringing up their children, or that their own upbringing, as males, has restricted their emotional development and capacity for intimacy.

While we may congratulate ourselves that, for example, women are allowed to own property, have the vote and may prosecute their husbands for rape within marriage, we should not assume that the future will be an uncomplicated story of increasing equality between the sexes, and moves toward equality have often been met by resistance. For example, under the Equal Pay Act, women doing the same work as men must be paid the same wage for it, and after the Act was passed employers were given a period of five years in which to bring their pay practices in line with it. However, in many cases this meant that the time was spent by employers in discovering ways in which the work performed by women could be defined as different from that of men, in order to allow them to continue paying women lower wages.

The social sciences therefore have an important role to play both in explaining gender differences and inequalities and in making recommendations for change. Clearly, the kinds of explanations that we come up with will have direct implications for our understanding of the possibilities and conditions for change. Whether and how we, as psychologists, might address gender inequalities depends upon our understanding of their relation to gender differences and gender relations. In other words, to what extent are gender inequalities based upon and sustained by gender differences (for example differences in personality) or by gender relations (for example marriage and heterosexuality)?

## Psychology and the study of gender

Psychology has not ignored these questions in the past, although it has been argued that its approach to them was not driven by a desire to combat inequality and did not escape the bounds of its own patriarchal assumptions (Gilligan 1977, 1982; Eisenstein, 1984; Squire 1989, 1990b). Psychology as a discipline and its handling of gender issues has been subjected to a critical feminist examination and found wanting. It is argued that psychology, like most academic disciplines, is dominated and run by men and reflects their interests and concerns. Academics, often themselves women, who wish to study issues more pertinent to women's experience often report that their male colleagues do not regard their work as worthwhile or academically respectable (e.g. Ussher's (1989) account of her work on menstruation).

It is also argued that male experience is assumed as the 'standard' to which the psychological processes of both sexes are compared. This means that where women's experience is different from that of men this difference is obscured. For example, studies of the psychological effects of unemployment or retirement have often used male samples. The effects described are therefore not really generalisable beyond male populations, but this limitation is often not articulated or noticed. In addition to marginalising women's experience in this way, it is further argued that psychological research has functioned to pathologise women and to find them lacking in some way. For example, Kohlberg (1969) developed a stage theory of moral thinking based upon longitudinal research using all-male samples. He later examined the moral thinking of both boys and girls, evaluating their responses to moral dilemmas. He used the stages of development that he had previously theorised and found that girls' moral thinking developmentally lagged behind that of boys (Kohlberg and Kramer, 1969). However, Gilligan (1977, 1982) has argued that the two sexes have different ways of assessing moral dilemmas, based upon their different life experiences, and that Kohlberg's stages, derived as they were from the responses of males, will inevitably distort and misrepresent women's moral thinking.

Psychology has traditionally described itself as apolitical. It has invested heavily in the idea of itself as an objective, value-free science and has therefore represented psychological findings as facts which are untainted by vested interests. This view has in recent times been seriously questioned (Sayers, 1982; Sherif, 1987). It is an issue which is wider in its implications than gender alone, and a full discussion of it is therefore not appropriate here, although I will say more about it in Chapter 6. We do not need to go as far as suggesting that psychologists have deliberately falsified their findings in order to satisfy the requirements of those funding the research, whether this be the government, the military or industry. It is sufficient to make the point that we only get answers to the questions that we ask and that it is the reasons why we ask some questions and not others that are informative about psychology's agenda. For example, nineteenth-century scientists found that women have smaller brains than men and argued that they therefore were unsuited to intellectual pursuits (Sayers, 1982). From the vantage point of the late twentieth century, we may see this as a thinly veiled political attempt to justify women's exclusion from education. But asking questions about relative brain size has only been superseded by questions about the effects of sex hormones on brain organisation (Moir and Jessel, 1989). The questions that are being asked appear to flow from an assumption that gender differences (and the inequalities linked to them) are 'hard-wired' in our biology, and thus more or less resistant to change.

Psychology's contribution to the study of gender has been concentrated in particular areas, and these too have come under attack. Of all the schools of psychological thought, **psychoanalysis** has had the most to say about gender and has been tremendously influential. According to Freud, children's gender identity rests on their recognition that they have (in the case of boys) or don't have (in the case of girls) a penis. For a boy, this is the symbol of his masculine identity. It is what guarantees that he will eventually take his rightful place in the powerful world of men. Both boys and girls are thought to believe that girls' lack of a penis is the result of having been castrated (perhaps for some wrong-doing in the past) and boys begin to live in fear of this happening to them too. During the Oedipal phase, when he is about three to five years old, the boy's increasing sexual awareness becomes directed toward his primary love object, his mother. But he fears that his more distant but powerful father, who is his rival for his mother's affections, will punish him for these feelings by castrating him. He resolves this conflict by repressing his feelings toward his mother and by identifying with his father, in the knowledge that if he becomes like him he too will eventually be able to establish a sexual relationship with another woman (instead of his mother). In identifying with his father, the boy internalises all that he stands for – the father's voice of authority and the social norms and mores that he embodies. This is why, Freud argues, men have a highly developed conscience and sense of idealism. By contrast girls, who are aware that their 'castrated' state renders them second class citizens, inevitably see their mothers as also castrated and therefore second best. In her identification with her mother, the girl then takes on board a submissive attitude in recognition of her own lower status. In addition, because she has not had to resolve the Oedipal conflict like her brother, she will never gain the strength of character, moral rectitude and idealism of a man.

Freud's account of gender clearly valorises masculinity and sees femininity as a very poor second. Many objections have been raised against Freud's views, which nevertheless have been very influential, particularly in medicine and psychiatry, and later feminist psychodynamic theorists have tried to produce psychoanalytic accounts which are not so misogynistic. First, it is argued that the awareness of genital differences may be only one, perhaps minor, factor in the production of gender identity. Furthermore, there seems no defensible reason why we should think of the male rather than the female genitals as superior. Freud just seemed to regard this as a fact rather than as a questionable assumption. A second criticism is that Freud assumes that the father is the primary agent of discipline in the home, whereas in many cases it may be the mother who performs this role. A third major criticism is that, like most psychological accounts, psychoanalytic theory seems to ignore gender as a system of power relations in society. It takes for granted men's relatively powerful position in the world and does not attempt to analyse the various instances of male domination such as domestic violence and child abuse.

Psychoanalysis itself has been heavily criticised from within psychology. As the discipline began to strive for a scientific image and reputation in the early part of this century, psychoanalysis came to be regarded as unscientific and untestable, and mainstream psychology instead took up with enthusiasm newer and more measurement-oriented approaches, in the form of **behaviourism** (which objectively studies how behaviours are acquired) and **psychometrics** (the development of measures and tests of psychological characteristics). Psychometrics has influenced the study of many areas of psychology, and gender is no exception. A major area of research grew up around the study of 'sex differences', which measured and documented the differences between women and men in a huge variety of characteristics and behaviours, and around the measurement of masculinity and femininity. However, as with psychoanalysis, gender was again viewed as a fundamentally psychological (rather than socio-psychological or cultural) phenomenon. Sex differences research has since been criticised for failing to interpret its findings from within a more social understanding of gender, and for uncritically accepting prevailing assumptions and **stereotypes** about the sexes (see Chapter 2), as has research into masculinity and femininity (see Chapter 6).

Psychology's contributions to the study of gender has therefore attracted a good deal of criticism, primarily for its ignorance and neglect of the social and political context of gender, and those working in the field today (often feminists) are more likely to have these matters at the forefront of their analyses.

## Key concepts and terms

From what I have said so far, it should be abundantly clear that gender is both a psychological and a social phenomenon. To study only its psychology, only its manifestation at the level of the individual person, is to artificially isolate it from the social, economic and political scene of which it is a part. To properly understand gender as psychologists we must be prepared to step outside of psychology, and so this book will continually weave the work of sociological and feminist writers into the psychological material. In this book and in others that you may read you will meet with a number of terms and concepts which may be unfamiliar to some, and I have therefore included a brief explanation and discussion of them here. The glossary on page 145 provides brief explanations of the technical terms and jargon that appear throughout the book.

**sex**   This is a biological term which refers to the particular chromosomes that are carried in the cells of the body. The twenty-third pair of chromosomes are the sex chromosomes, either XX (female) or XY (male) and (normally) produce the two different patterns of physical development that we associate with men and women. The letters roughly describe the shape of the chromosomes.

**gender**   Gender is the social significance of sex. It refers to the constellation of characteristics and behaviours which come to be differentially associated with and expected of men and women in a particular society, our notions of masculinity and femininity. Such differences may really exist, or they may be only supposed to exist.

**sex differences**   This usually refers to the body of research which has tried to assess the nature and extent of psychological differences between the sexes. An extensive and classic study in this field was carried out by Maccoby and Jacklin (1974).

**sex roles**   'Role' is a sociological term borrowed, as you might guess, from the theatre. It refers to the set of behaviours, duties and expectations attached to occupying a particular social position, like 'priest' or 'police officer'. 'Sex roles' therefore refer to the ways we expect women and men to behave. However, role also has an interactional element, and implies reciprocity. You can't carry off your role as, say, a 'teacher' without others who are prepared to take up the role of 'student'. So sex roles are also about the ways that the behavioural scripts for women and men are played out with respect to each other.

**gender division of labour**   There are a number of ways in which the work that women and men do is apportioned. The 'vertical gender division of labour' refers to the fact that men are more likely than women to occupy high status, well paid, secure jobs. The 'horizontal gender division of labour' refers to the way that the range of jobs and careers is patterned according to gender. Jobs in the service industries and caring professions are women's jobs and those in industry and commerce are men's jobs, both in terms of how these jobs are perceived and in terms of the actual numbers of women and men employed in them. The 'gender division of labour' also refers to the separation of work in the public sphere from work in the home, with women being associated primarily with the latter and men with the former.

**gender differentiation** The exaggeration or creation of differences between females and males, where no natural differences exist (for example through colour-coded clothing for babies, hairstyles, his and hers versions of personal items etc.).

**sex discrimination** This means treating people less favourably (for example by paying them less or allowing them fewer rights) on the basis of their sex. In practice, this is usually taken to mean discrimination against women. However, it can certainly be argued that there are areas where men are discriminated against on the basis of their sex. For example, men have historically been at a disadvantage in child custody cases, they are less likely to have the right to paid leave from employment on the birth of a child, and can be required by the state to fight in times of war. Of course not all men would necessarily see these differences in treatment as disadvantageous to them.

**femininity and masculinity** These refer to the social and cultural expectations attached to being a woman or a man, and cover all aspects of our thinking and behaviour, our aspirations, our appearance and so on. Because they are developed or constructed socially, that is they are produced and reproduced by people who share a culture, they are not fixed but vary across time and place. For example, it is often pointed out that the traditional feminine beauty portrayed in the paintings of Rubens would today be seen as too obese to be attractive. Also the desirable tanned skin of today was deplored by women a century ago, and would have been seen as coarse and unladylike. The examples are useful because they illustrate how notions of acceptable femininity are tied to economic conditions and the distribution of wealth (the availability of sufficient food and the necessity, or lack of it, of labouring in the fields). Today, writers are more likely to reject the idea that there is one, unified version of what it means to be a woman or a man in contemporary society. In recent years, for example, there has been a move toward talking of a plurality of masculinities, to describe the various models of acceptably being a man that are currently available for men to adopt and live out.

**essentialism**   The idea that human beings have an essence or fixed nature that is expressed in their behaviour. Essentialism lies behind the claim that there is such a thing as a 'human nature' that we can, in principle, discover and which is more or less consistent across time and cultures. It also lies behind the claim that people behave in the way that they do because of the kind of person they are (for example 'introverted', 'outgoing' or 'neurotic'). Essentialism looks for entities or structures inside of the person to explain their behaviour. In gender, it takes the form of the view that there is a definable female or male nature which is expressed in differences in personality, job preferences, desire for parenthood etc. This essential nature is often, but not necessarily, seen as biologically determined.

**reductionism**   Human social phenomena may be analysed at a number of levels of explanation. In the social sciences, these are frequently the biological, psychological and societal levels. It is therefore possible to look at, say, the fact that women are primarily responsible for childcare and offer (at least) three kinds of explanations: they are programmed to do so by their genes or hormones (biology), they have the desire to do so and the personality characteristics best suited to the task (psychological) or they are effectively given no choice in the matter, since their access to paid work is limited (societal). Reductionist arguments line up these different levels in a causative chain and reduce them all down to one level. In the example above a reductionist argument would be that women are more likely to be found in the domestic sphere (social) because they are more nurturant than men (psychological) and this nurturance originates in turn in genetic or hormonal processes (biological). Reductionist arguments very often operate in this direction, although there is no reason why the line of causation should not work in the opposite direction (women's position and experience in society moulds them into certain kinds of people and these psychological processes influence their hormone production).

**feminism**   Those who call themselves feminists are generally seeking for women and men to enjoy the same opportunities, privileges and rights. Feminism is committed to theorising the bases of inequality and to a programme of social change for addressing it. There are of course different views as to why there is gender inequality, giving rise to different forms of feminism with different recommendations for change.

**patriarchy**   Literally, this means 'rule by the father'. Historically, the term was used to refer to a system of government in which older men governed women and younger men through their position as heads of households. Today, the term is usually rather more loosely used to describe systematic power inequalities between women and men. For this reason some writers use the term 'andrarchy' instead (meaning 'rule by men'). Walby defines patriarchy as 'a system of social structures and practices in which men dominate, oppress and exploit women' (Walby, 1990: 20).

## Feminist theories

Throughout the book I will be drawing on a number of psychological and feminist theoretical perspectives in order to offer an analysis of various gender phenomena. You will probably already know something about psychological theories such as behaviourism, **social learning theory** and psychodynamic theory, but will be less familiar with feminist theories, and I therefore include here a brief account of these.

As I pointed out earlier, feminists differ in their analysis of the causes of gender inequalities and therefore in their recommendations for change. There are therefore now a number of different forms of feminism, each focusing upon somewhat different aspects of gender. However, nearly all forms of feminism regard gender inequalities as produced by factors in the social environment and in no way natural. They therefore usually occupy the nurture side of the nature–nurture debate. I have included here those that you are most likely to meet in other books on the subject. Throughout the book, I shall be drawing upon these in order to examine the implications of the psychological theory and research that I shall be discussing.

### Liberal feminism

Liberal feminism can be traced back historically to the increasing importance placed upon individual human rights and freedoms that occurred during the eighteenth century. Liberal feminists begin with the assertion that as human beings women have a natural right to the same opportunities and freedoms as men, and their approach has been to fight for these by campaigning for changes in laws which discriminated against women. As well as campaigning to gain rights for women which were previously only enjoyed by men (as in the women's suffrage movement) they also campaigned against laws which discriminated against women but which were claimed to be for their protection. For example, a number of Factory Acts passed in the nineteenth century excluded women from night work and limited their working hours to ten hours per day. These provisions became embodied in later acts passed in this century, and are largely still in effect today. Oakley (1981a) suggests that such laws in reality prevent women from full participation in paid work and would be seen as indefensible if they were applied to, say, ethnic groups.

In terms of their theoretical analysis of gender inequalities, liberal feminists see the root of the problem as lying in the way that children are socialised. They see gender inequalities as resting upon differences between the sexes (for example in their capabilities, aptitudes, aspirations and so on) that are acquired or learned as they grow up. These differences may well be quite real (rather than only being imagined to exist) but they are in no way inevitable. Liberal feminists assume that girls and boys are born with equal potential to develop a variety of skills and abilities and that it is only through our child-rearing practices and educational practices that they learn to become typically feminine or masculine. The liberal feminist solution therefore is to concentrate upon changing our attitudes and ideas about gender, for example through changes in educational practices and materials.

For psychology, there are important questions to be addressed. To what extent do the personality differences that are said to exist between the sexes really exist? How do girls and boys come to take on the abilities, preferences and behaviours that are seen as appropriate to their sex? How can we change how people think about women and men, and will it make a difference to how they are treated?

Liberal feminism has, however, been criticised for ignoring the way that the world is produced and dominated by male concerns and interests. For example, it could be argued from a liberal feminist perspective that women should have the same opportunities as men to follow a career in which commitment to the job must take priority over every other concern (such as children or friends). However, many would argue that rather than claim for women the same problems that are visited upon men, we should concentrate upon changing our social arrangements in ways which are more beneficial to both sexes.

### *Marxist feminism*

The fundamental problem, for Marxist feminists, is capitalism. According to Marx, under a capitalist economic system, the owners of the means of production (the middle class owners of factories and businesses) exploit their workers (the working class) by paying them a wage which is less than the value of the work that they do and keeping the difference for themselves (the profit). But the lynchpin of this operation is the normal heterosexual family where women are said to reproduce the labour force.

This reproduction has two facets to it – the daily renewal of the (male) worker by caring for his physical needs (preparing food for him, washing his clothes, looking after him when he is sick) and the replacement of workers through giving birth to, caring for and bringing up the next generation of employees. Women are not paid to do this work, and this is vital for capitalism to be sustained. If wives refused to do such work, it would have to be done by others who were paid to do it (housekeepers, nurses etc.) and these costs would be passed on to the employers through the necessary higher wages that would be needed to cover the cost of living, thus taking away the profit.

Women's location in the private, domestic sphere and their relatively restricted access to **paid work** are therefore, for Marxist feminists, caused by capitalism and it is therefore capitalism that must be eradicated if women are to gain equality. Unlike radical feminists (see p. 18) Marxist feminists see *capitalism* and not *men* as the prime cause and beneficiary of gender inequality. However, from a psychological standpoint the interesting question is how

17

this exploitative sleight of hand is achieved. If we ask women why they get married and care for their husbands and children they are unlikely to reply: 'In order to support capitalism'. The task of psychology is therefore to cast some light upon how women come to desire marriage and a family and how men come to derive their sense of self in part from their job or career.

Marxist feminism has, however, been criticised for having an inadequate account of the subordination of women in precapitalist societies. It also cannot really explain why it is women who provide domestic labour in the home. We might accept that capitalism needs people to do this work, but why women? Some Marxist feminists, such as Michelle Barratt, have suggested that capitalism is not the only important factor. She argues that the ideology of family life pre-existed capitalism and then became taken up and used by it. For Barratt it is therefore gender relations in the family which are fundamental to gender inequality and have become intertwined with capitalism since industrialisation. The difference in emphasis is the crucial difference between Marxist feminism and radical feminism, which sees relations between women and men (rather than between the middle and working classes) as the root of gender problems.

### Radical feminism

It is radical feminism which places the concept of 'patriarchy' at the centre of its theorising. Radical feminists claim that women as a class are and probably always have been dominated and controlled by men as a class, and that this domination and control pervades all aspects of our lives. So that it is not only in the sphere of paid work and in the relation between the public and domestic spheres that women are oppressed, but also in all their private relations with men. This includes their personal relationships with them, their child-bearing and rearing in the family, sexual relations including rape, prostitution and **sexual harassment**. Radical feminism gave rise to the phrase 'the personal is political', because it refused to see gender inequalities as located only in the arena of public life and paid work.

A potent issue for radical feminists is the role that biology plays in producing and structuring these oppressive relations between the sexes. Some see women's reproductive role as central, while others concentrate on the variety of forms that male violence toward women takes. Yet others have concentrated upon the way that a masculine view of the world (sometimes referred to as 'malestream', to reflect the way that 'male' is also 'mainstream') has marginalised and distorted women's experience. For example, it is claimed that science (including psychology), as a male institution, has been used to shore up the ideologies that define women as inferior.

The questions raised by radical feminism, while coming from a sociological base, are of immense interest to the psychologist. These are questions about the biological bases of sexuality, mothering and family life, about how we should theorise homosexuality and lesbianism, about the origins of the division of labour in the home and about the causes of rape and domestic violence. Radical feminism has also been largely responsible for the growth in 'feminist research' which is impacting upon psychology and other social sciences by questioning its methods and practices and by encouraging research which is both about and *for* women. For example, they advocate consciousness-raising, where women talk to each other about the experience of being a woman and in so doing become aware of their oppression.

### Socialist feminism

This is sometimes referred to as dual systems theory because it insists that neither capitalism nor patriarchy alone can explain gender inequalities. Socialist feminists therefore understand gender in terms of the way the two systems, the economic system and the system of gender relations, interact with each other. They see patriarchy as transcending time and culture, and therefore recognise that it existed before capitalism. And yet, with the advent of capitalism, patriarchy took on a particular form. Socialist feminists therefore argue that the specific form that patriarchy takes, that is the particular ways in which men as a class have power over women as a class, will depend upon the economic system currently operating in a society. For example, before industrialisation, patriarchy could be seen as rooted in the private domain, where individual women were subordinate to individual men in the household (their fathers and husbands). With industrialisation, the focus of patriarchy has arguably moved into the public sphere, where women are subordinate to men in the labour market.

Walby (1990) argues that what has happened here is that the move away from a home-based economy toward capitalism resulted in a shift in the power resources available to men. Because of their pre-existing relatively powerful positions with respect to women, they were already well-placed to develop new power bases as the face of the economy, and their place in it, changed.

Socialist feminists argue that, to properly understand women's oppression, we must look at both the gender division of labour in the domestic sphere as well as in paid work and understand how they are related. This means looking at how marriage and family life functions to limit women's access to paid work and how their lower level of pay in turn keeps women dependent upon marriage as a way of supporting themselves financially. The ideology of marriage and motherhood is seen as concealing this mechanism.

This is not to say that patriarchy and capitalism always work together hand in hand. They are two different systems of oppression and sometimes have conflicting interests. In particular, they may pull in opposite directions over the exploitation of women's labour. It is in the interests of capitalism to draft women into the labour force because their labour is cheap, but it is in the interests of patriarchy to retain them in the home, servicing men.

From a psychological standpoint, these issues become played out in interesting ways. Women who desire (or must combine) both paid work and a family often experience conflict in their attempts to live up to their own expectations and those of others. The allocation of domestic tasks is now a hot potato for many couples, and there is much debate over why men are less likely than women to be found performing household or childcare duties. Many people are questioning the ground rules of traditional forms of marriage and family life. Women who choose a career rather than motherhood must deal with the consequences of having in effect troubled the images and expectations of traditional femininity and womanliness. Likewise, men who choose to become househusbands must find a way of being men that is socially acceptable.

### Black feminism

Gender inequality is of course not the only inequality suffered by people, and recent feminist writing has been concerned to point out both that many people suffer multiple oppressions (for example, they may be black, working class and disabled in addition to being female), and that oppression and inequality are experienced in different ways depending upon one's location in other divisions like class and ethnicity. Black feminism argues that the feminisms developed largely in response to the problems of white, middle class women do not encompass and explain the experience of all women and argues that feminism ought to explicitly examine the relation between gender and ethnicity. In addition to challenging capitalism and patriarchy, racism must also be addressed. In terms of research, black feminism has studied the experiences of black women in the family, education and work.

### Overview of other chapters

*Chapter 2* Gender differences in personality: sex differences research; the nature–nurture debate; the role of biology; **socialisation**, social learning theory and **gender roles**; gender development and moral development; sexuality and aggression.

*Chapter 3* Education: gender differences in educational attainment and subject choice; the hidden curriculum; educational materials; teachers' attitudes and expectations; gender relations and interactions in the school; feminist analyses of gender in education; initiatives for change.

*Chapter 4*   Work and family: the gender division of labour in employment, the **domestic gender division of labour** and the relationship between these; the role of reproduction and parenting; psychological and feminist explanations.

*Chapter 5*   Representations and language: representations of gender in television, children's reading material and women's magazines; masculinity, femininity and sexuality in visual representations of women and men; pornography; gender, language and political correctness; **social constructionism, discourse** and identity.

*Chapter 6*   Gender and psychological research: sex differences research; measuring masculinity and femininity; androgyny and a feminist critique; 'malestream' psychology; value-freedom and objectivity in psychology and psychology as political; rewriting the aims of research; feminist research and tensions between feminism and psychology.

## Summary

I have shown how gender, in a multitude of ways, infiltrates our lives in often subtle ways. I have outlined some of the major inequalities that are considered to exist between women and men, and suggested that these inequalities may be intimately connected to the various psychological differences that are in evidence in everyday normal activities. In order to address these inequalities and offer recommendations for change we need to examine the relationship between gendered psychological processes and gendered societal arrangements. I have outlined some of the important questions for psychology, but also pointed out that psychology has been criticised for itself contributing to gender problems. In order to properly locate the psychology of gender in its social, economic and political context, a number of feminist theories have been introduced and will be referred to throughout the book.

## Further reading

Bryson, V. (1992) *Feminist Political Theory: An Introduction*, Basingstoke: Macmillan. A British text tracing the different strands of feminism through history from the seventeenth century.

*Polity Reader in Gender Studies* (1994), Cambridge: Polity Press. A wide-ranging collection of papers giving a taster of a number of gender issues.

Tong, R. (1989) *Feminist Thought: A Comprehensive Introduction*, London: Routledge. A very readable American text, giving an account of the major feminist theories.

# Chapter 2

## Gender differences in personality

I T IS OFTEN CLAIMED that women and men are different kinds of people, with different abilities and aptitudes, different patterns of personality characteristics, different behaviours and different emotional capacities. This is both a common sense view, held by many ordinary people, and also a view held by some psychologists. It is an important issue because gender differences in personality are often assumed to lie behind (and cause) the gender inequalities that we see around us. There are two questions to be addressed here. First, are women and men in fact as different as they are commonly supposed? And second, if we find that these differences are real, how do we account for them? It is important to be clear that these two questions are independent of each other. It is sometimes (wrongly) assumed that if we take the view that there are real differences between women and men, that we are also saying that these differences are inevitable and must have their roots in our biology. To say that gender differences are real is to leave open the question of how they originated. Furthermore, the question of the existence (or not) of gender differences in personality is analysed, by traditional psychology, within a fundamentally individualistic framework. Differences between people (and between the sexes) are thought of as emanating from within them as individuals (perhaps through the operation of personality traits or genetic tendencies). As I pointed out in Chapter 1, psychology has defined itself as the study of individuals and has been reluctant to consider the role of a person's social context in producing their behaviour and experience. Although this individualism has recently been challenged by critical social psychologists (e.g. Shotter, 1990; Sampson, 1990) the majority of psychological research and theory regarding gender differences has been socially 'blinkered'.

## Sex differences research

Since the turn of the century 'sex differences' have been extensively researched by psychologists (I have used the term 'sex' rather than 'gender' here as this is the term used in the literature). The nature of this research reflects the rise in popularity of laboratory **experiments** and psychometrics in psychology generally. (Psychometrics is the branch of psychology which deals with the development of scales and inventories for the measurement of psychological characteristics and phenomena). An enormous range of behaviours and characteristics have been compared across the sexes, using a plethora of scales, inventories and questionnaires. Just a few examples from this list are sensory capacities and attention in infancy, reaction to frustration, timidity, verbal and spatial skills, memory, cognitive style, creativity, achievement motivation, risk-taking, social behaviour, self-concept, dependency, aggression, dominance and compliance. It is worth making the point that this enthusiastic attempt to leave no stone unturned in the search for sex differences possibly says more about our commitment to the belief that women and men are different kinds of people than about those differences themselves.

However, this wealth of data has not produced unequivocal evidence. Sex differences research is a sprawling, uncoordinated affair with no obvious research direction, and this is in part due to the fact that many of the sex differences reported in the literature are secondary findings in research designed to answer quite different questions. There have been relatively few attempts to review this mass of research findings in order to try to discern any common themes, but of those who have tried, the work of Maccoby and Jacklin (1974) is probably the most well known. They reviewed the evidence from an enormous variety of research studies covering a wide range of behaviours, characteristics and abilities. They concluded that there was probably enough evidence to support the argument that females and males are different kinds of people in just four areas:

1   Verbal ability: as girls grow up, they become more verbally competent than boys as measured by tests of fluency, comprehension, creative writing and so on.

2   Visual–spatial ability: as boys grow up, they become better than girls at visual–spatial tasks such as the Embedded Figures Test, the Rod and Frame Test, and identifying rotated figures.

3   Mathematical ability: again, beginning around age 12, boys overtake girls in their mathematical ability. However, many researchers have argued that this advantage is likely to be due to the pay-offs of boys' greater visual–spatial ability in mathematical problems that involve graph-reading or geometry, and therefore feel that mathematical ability should not be counted as a separate sex difference.

4   Aggressiveness: this was the clearest difference identified. From early childhood, boys were found to be more verbally and physically aggressive than girls and to engage more frequently in mock-fighting and aggressive fantasies.

Maccoby and Jacklin conclude that there is inadequate research evidence for many of the differences evident in popular stereotypes of women and men. In the four areas above they found fairly small but consistent differences, and they argue that sex differences have been systematically exaggerated and similarities minimised. In general, there was a great deal of overlap between females and males on the dimensions studied, with the possibility that differences between women or between men may be as great as between the sexes.

## Problems with sex differences research

There are a number of reasons why we should view sex differences research findings with caution.

In very many cases, the significant differences that are reported are due to the large numbers of subjects in the study. Very small differences in numerical measures reach significance when that difference is consistent across a large sample, so that even if some sex differences are statistically significant the rather small actual size of the difference may render it quite uninteresting psychologically. It has also been pointed out that when we are looking at large numbers of research studies, as we are here, then chance alone would lead us to expect a certain proportion of significant findings.

There is a considerable general tendency among researchers to report findings of statistical significance and to fail to report findings where no difference was established. In sex differences research this leads to an exaggerated impression of the extent of the differences between women and men. The body of research evidence as a whole is therefore tuned in to difference rather than similarity. Many later writers, particularly feminists, take this view. But there are others (e.g. Eagly, 1983) who, on the contrary, claim that anomalies in the analysis of existing research findings have masked real differences between the sexes. Not all feminists believe that women and men are 'naturally' more similar than different. For example, Mary Daly (1979, 1984), a radical feminist, argues that women have an essential femininity, a way of looking at and living in the world which is better than that of men.

There are often problems in defining or operationalising concepts for measurement in both experimental and naturalistic studies. For example, operational definitions of aggressive behaviour varied considerably in the studies reviewed by Maccoby and Jacklin. In one case aggression was taken as 'throwing, hitting with an object or pushing', in a second 'choosing an aggressive toy' and in a third 'using hostile verbs following **vicarious reinforcement**'. We cannot be sure that these studies are all measuring the same thing, and different people may disagree upon what counts as aggressive behaviour.

Given the extent and prevalence of assumptions about women and men in contemporary society we should not be surprised if findings are interpreted in the direction of existing stereotypes. For example, in studies in which children were left alone in a room with an attractive toy which they had been told by the experimenter not to touch, it has often been found that girls are less likely to touch the toy or refrain from touching it for longer than boys (Parke, 1967; Stouwie, 1971). This difference has been interpreted in terms of the greater obedience or compliance of girls, but it might just as legitimately have been suggested that girls have a greater respect for others' property or that both girls and boys are aware that, if they are caught being naughty, adults are likely to be more tolerant of (and even subtly encourage) misbehaviour in boys.

As with all laboratory studies, there is the issue of whether taking the behaviour out of its natural context strips it of its meaning. Much of our behaviour is heavily dependent upon its social context (it is 'situation-specific'), and we might expect children's aggressiveness, helpfulness or timidity to vary depending on whether they are at home, school or in the local park, and upon who else is present or watching. This is not to say that we should ignore the findings of sex differences research. Clearly, the findings relating to aggression would seem to be borne out by a variety of phenomena occurring in social life. For example, football hooliganism, domestic violence, rape and other violent crimes are committed predominantly by men. Differences in spatial and verbal abilities are consistent with gendered subject choices in higher education. The Equal Opportunities Commission (EOC) reports that in 1994/5 there were one and a half times as many women undergraduates as men studying languages, and over six times as many men as women studying engineering and technology.

Despite these cautions, it seems reasonable to accept that women and men differ in some psychological characteristics. It is also hard to ignore the claims about difference that arise from our common experience of social life. It is often said that women and men differ in their emotional capacities, with women finding it much easier than men to establish intimate relationships and to talk about their feelings. This is linked to the observation that women's and men's friendships often have different foundations. Women are more likely to say that their friendships involve talking about personal issues and discussing relationship matters, whereas men are more likely to base their friendships upon joint activities (like sport) and on less intimate topics of conversation (see

Nardi, 1992). It is sometimes claimed that these emotional and relational differences underlie the apparent difference between the sexes in their desire for and involvement in caring for children, and women's greater visibility in the caring professions.

## The nature–nurture debate

If we accept that women and men are in fact different in at least some psychological characteristics, how can we account for these differences? As with some other notable aspects of our psychology, such as intelligence, the answers to this question have often been framed by what is referred to as the nature–nurture debate. Is our behaviour and psychological make-up determined by biological mechanisms, such as genes and hormones, or is it the product of environmental influences? At present, the commonly accepted view is that both biology and environment interact in complex ways to produce the psychological and social phenomena we experience, and claims that our psychology is either completely determined by biology or by the environment are rare. Nevertheless, it is fair to say that the claims of the effects of 'nurture' have often been made in response to and in reaction against those of the claims of 'nature'. When the behaviourist J.B. Watson made his famous statement claiming that it would be possible to produce any kind of human being we wish through manipulating her/his environment, he did so while explicitly stating that the extremity of his claim was an attempt to redress the balance:

> I am going far beyond my facts and I admit it, but so have the advocates of the contrary and they have been doing it for many thousands of years.

> (Watson, 1930: 104)

The nature–nurture debate is anything but a purely academic issue. As a society, our decisions and policies regarding educational performance, crime, physical and mental health and a host of other issues are deeply affected by our beliefs about their biological and environmental determinants. The debate is

31

therefore a highly political one. Although many accept an inter-actionist position, there is a common sense assumption (which may have no factual basis) that biological factors exert a powerful 'push' in particular directions, and that (weaker) environmental influences have a merely moderating effect. Biological influences are assumed to be deeper and stronger than societal forces, which are seen as more superficial. It is significant that the study of the biological sciences has often seemed somehow more relevant to the education of psychologists than has sociology. This may in part be due to biology's longer history as a science, but it is also a symptom of the ubiquitous biological reductionism that can be identified in our everyday common sense accounts as well as in psychology

Interestingly, there is a marked current trend toward discovering strong genetic influences upon a variety of psychological and social phenomena, including alcoholism, mental illness, crime and homosexuality, as well as gender. In the light of our propensity for viewing biological forces as powerful and their effects as immutable, this trend gives rise to some worrying implications and we may do well to remind ourselves of the political driving force behind the eugenics research of the early twentieth century and the uses to which the research findings were put. Given that biological accounts have often been used to support and legitimate inegalitarian practices (Sayers, 1982), many feminists have understandably been keen to develop fully social accounts of gender differences, and this move has been welcomed by like-minded psychologists. This has led to a rise in psychological publications which explicitly reject the traditional psychological approach to gender, such as the relatively new journal *Feminism and Psychology*.

## The role of biology

In addition to the assumption that biology is a more powerful force than society, there is also a marked tendency to value the natural over the cultural. This is a reversal of the nineteenth

century view which celebrated the attempts of humanity to manip-
ulate nature and in which our 'natural' drives and predispositions
were cause for regret. In contemporary western society the natural
has come to acquire not only a positive aesthetic value but also
a moral value. What is natural is also what is right. For example,
those who do not accept homosexuality as a legitimate way of
life often argue that it is unnatural, and clearly feel that to demonstrate this is also to demonstrate its unacceptability. Similarly,
claims of the naturalness of gender differences have acquired a
moral imperative – if women and men are naturally different,
these differences must be right. However, we can see that nature
is mobilised in arguments for ideological purposes. Wearing
clothes, cultivating garden plants or going to the opera could
hardly be seen as natural human activities but few would claim
that they are morally indefensible.

Biological accounts of gender differences have focused upon
hormonal, genetic and evolutionary factors. They are deterministic
and reductionistic, positing a causal route from biological through
psychological to societal phenomena. Thus, biological events such
as genetic endowment and hormone activity are seen as producing
psychological differences between the sexes such as differences in
aggressiveness or nurturance, which in their turn give rise to social
phenomena such as domestic violence or the horizontal and vertical
divisions of labour. The status of these phenomena as biologically
driven and the observation that 'things have always been that way'
is then often used to claim that they are therefore desirable or at
least unchangeable.

### Hormonal accounts

These accounts are of various kinds. Some claim that the sex
hormones (androgen, progesterone and oestrogen) have a direct
effect upon our thinking and behaviour. For example, the mood
changes that are said to affect women during their menstrual cycle
are assumed to result from changes in hormone levels in the blood.
However, Ussher (1989) points out that research has not demonstrated a clear relationship between mood and hormone levels.

Evidence relating aggressiveness to androgen and testosterone levels has come mainly from animal studies (primarily using rats), with consequent difficulties for generalising to human samples, and where human subjects have been used the evidence is contradictory. For example, Persky *et al.* (1971) found a positive correlation between aggressive and hostile feelings (measured by several psychological tests) and testosterone levels in a sample of young men. Likewise, Kling (1975), using a sample of prisoners, found that those in the most 'aggressive' group had higher testosterone levels. However, several other studies using prisoners (Kreuz and Rose, 1972), college students (Meyer-Bahlberg *et al.*, 1974) and psychiatric inpatients (Rose, 1975) found no relationship between measures of aggression or hostility and testosterone levels (see Archer and Lloyd, 1985 and Fausto-Sterling, 1985 for overviews). Numerous studies have looked at unusual cases where the foetus has been exposed to opposite sex hormones. However, the evidence is again contradictory and such studies often suffer from methodological inadequacies.

Increasingly popular are theories which claim that hormones influence the developing brains of female and male children, producing differences in brain specialisation. Specifically, exposure of the foetal brain to androgens (male hormones) is said to produce a greater degree of specialisation in the male brain. In men, the right hemisphere (which controls visual–spatial activities) is dominant, whereas in women it is the left (controlling verbal abilities), and men's brains show a greater degree of specialisation. In their popular book *Brain Sex*, Moir and Jessel (1989) argue that this specialisation accounts for familiar gender differences. For example, because of their greater specialisation, men's emotional and verbal centres are unconnected to each other, making it difficult for them to talk about their feelings.

The differential specialisation of female and male brains is also said to account for educational and career choices, so that the right-hemisphere dominated male brain gives men superior spatial abilities suitable for architecture or engineering, while left-hemisphere dominated women acquire good verbal abilities suitable for the study of languages. Such explanations may sound convincing, but they make a huge leap in simply mapping complex social phenomena onto biological processes in this way, and it is worth asking whether, if there is a causal relationship between brain organisation and gender differences, it might operate in the reverse direction with emerging patterns of behaviour and interest in girls and boys influencing brain specialisation.

### Genetic and evolutionary accounts

As technological advances have made it possible to conduct more sophisticated research on genetic material, accounts claiming the discovery of genes said to control a variety of human attributes and behaviours have flourished. With respect to gender, this has focused upon the claim that aggressiveness in males is genetically endowed. In addition, the concepts of natural and sexual selection, which form the basis of the theory of evolution, have been used in conjunction with this to produce **sociobiological** accounts of gender differences and gendered social organisation. The findings of studies of children where anatomical anomalies have led to mis-identification of their sex at birth (e.g. Money and Ehrhardt, 1972) are notoriously difficult to interpret, and genetic research generally would suggest that the idea that there is a single gene responsible for even relatively straightforward characteristics such as hair colour, let alone for complex social behaviours, is too simplistic.

Nevertheless, despite the fact that the evidence regarding the heritability of aggressiveness is by no means clear, the appeal of sociobiological accounts has been considerable. Sociobiological accounts begin from the observations that, in most animal species, the male appears to be more aggressive than the female and is more sexually promiscuous, and that in most hunter-gatherer societies (from which contemporary industrial societies are thought to have evolved) the men do the hunting and the women stay closer to home and are occupied in nursing and rearing children. (Incidentally, the great importance of the food-gathering that the women did is often overlooked in our fascination with what we see as the excitement and adventure of the hunting side of the equation). In such societies, sociobiologists argue, a sexual division of labour would be highly functional. Women, encumbered by frequent pregnancies and the need to care for young children, would have been unsuited to hunting, which would also have endangered their offspring. Men who were rather more aggressive than their peers would have been more successful at hunting and defending themselves, and it is these men who would survive to pass on their genes to the next generation. Likewise, women who were rather more nurturant than others would be more likely to see their offspring survive to reproduce in their turn. Therefore the process of natural selection (survival of the fittest) produces and reproduces highly functional sex differences.

Thus, males have become genetically programmed for aggressiveness and females for nurturance. These genetic predispositions are thought to operate through evolved differences in brain structure and functions and through hormone activity, and manifest themselves in the psychological and social differences we see between the sexes. According to one of the originators of sociobiology, E.O. Wilson, these differences are functional for society and resistant to change by social interventions:

> even in the most free and most egalitarian of future societies, men are likely to continue to play a disproportionate role in political life, business and science.
>
> (Wilson, 1975)

According to sociobiology, male aggressiveness and promiscuity have also emerged via a second evolutionary process, that of sexual selection. The survival of any animal species depends in part upon individual females and males choosing mates who will produce good, strong offspring. The task of the female is therefore to find a mate whose genes will give their offspring a good chance of survival. This is an important choice for the female, because she will be pregnant with and have to nurse the child for a considerable time, and this involves a high investment of her energies. In addition, her opportunities to produce new offspring are relatively infrequent compared to the male, due to the length of the gestation period and cycles of fertility. There is therefore a logic in females being choosy about their mates. However, for the male, whose investment of energy in the reproduction process is minimal, there is no such need. On the contrary, it would seem sensible for the male to try to impregnate as many females as possible in order to give his genes the best chance of being passed on to the next generation.

But how is the female to recognise a good male? In many animal societies the males, through fighting and challenging each other, form themselves into a dominance hierarchy, and it is usually the males at the top who have the best chance of mating with a female. Not only are the stronger, more aggressive males able to discourage their rivals, but the females know that these males, being themselves good survivors are likely to produce strong offspring. However, in addition to passing on to their offspring genes which will give them advantages in terms of size, strength, resistance to disease and so on, these males are also passing on their propensity for pugnacity and dominance, which allowed them to reach the top of the hierarchy in the first place. Thus aggressiveness in males becomes genetically programmed, and their promiscuity is a survival mechanism. Sociobiology claims that these mechanisms are just as relevant to understanding contemporary western industrialised societies as animal societies or hunter-gatherer societies. The survival of the species depends upon them, although there are some negative side effects of these processes in terms of men's driving ambition and ruthlessness, violent crime and rape. Understandably, these ideas have provoked some fierce opposition, since they not only portray male aggressiveness and sexual exploitation as natural and therefore unavoidable, but also imply that their survival value makes them desirable.

These biological accounts are extreme forms of reductionism and **determinism,** and the pity is that most biological accounts within psychology have this flavour. In rejecting their reductionism and determinism we are by default rejecting virtually all existing accounts of the relationship between biology and gender. While I believe that it is a mistake to imagine that we can reduce complex social phenomena to biological mechanisms, on the other hand

37

to try to explain human behaviour and experience without reference to our physical embodiment is also inadequate. Rose *et al.* (1990) take a commendably cautious position:

> although all future as well as past forms of relationship between men and women, both individually and within society as a whole, must be in accord with human biology, we have no way of deducing from the diversity of human history and anthropology or from human biology or from the study of ethology of non-human species the constraints, if any, that such a statement imposes.
>
> (Rose *et al.*, 1990: 162)

Our size and shape, bodily processes and physical abilities must, in the process of our engagement with the physical and social world, surely frame and help to produce our psychological experience. However, theoretical attempts to elaborate this engagement are generally lacking.

## The role of socialisation

Socialisation refers to the processes by which people come to adopt the behaviours deemed appropriate in their culture. It is usually used in relation to children, who gradually learn to adopt the behaviour appropriate to and acceptable in a variety of different social situations, but it should not be forgotten that our socialisation never actually ends. Even as adults our behaviour is continually moderated by social pressures and expectations.

### Cross-cultural comparisons

If personality differences and differences between women and men in their participation in society (often referred to as gender roles) were simply an outcome of biological predispositions, we would expect to find the same gender differences and divisions of labour in all human societies. Studies of other cultures have shown that this is not the case, and therefore suggest that gender

differences and roles are acquired through socialisation processes. Malinowski's (1932) famous anthropological study of the
Trobriand Islanders found them to have a very different conception of appropriate male and female sexuality to our own. Mead
(1935) studied three tribes in New Guinea, and found they
differed both from each other and from western societies in the
way that personality was gendered. The Arapesh valued gentle-
ness, caring and child-centredness in adults of both sexes, whereas
the Mun-dug-u-mor women and men were equally vigorous, independent and assertive. Among the Tchambuli, the women were
self-assertive and managing, while the men wore ornaments and
were interested in gossip. Although in virtually all human societies there is a gender division of labour, with women's jobs and
men's jobs, the content of these roles varies, with women often
carrying out tasks requiring heavy physical labour. Although
numerous cross-cultural studies have been carried out, many of
them were conducted a long time ago and are now often subjected
to methodological criticisms which raise questions about the
interpretation of their findings. It is probably true to say that,
depending upon what argument one is trying to support, it is
possible to produce from cross-cultural studies evidence of both
similarities and differences between cultures. Nevertheless, our
own localised view, from within our own particular culture, of
what women and men are like does not appear to be a universal
one.

### Gender development

Children gradually acquire the concept of gender, suggesting that
gender identity is not something which they naturally have.
Kohlberg (1966), a cognitive developmental theorist, argued that
children come to be able to understand the world in terms of
categories, including gender categories, as their intellectual abilities develop. Between the ages of two and five years children come
to realise that people are categorised by sex, that you can only
belong to one category, and that you can't (normally) change the
category you belong to. Research evidence supports this, showing

that most children can correctly answer the question 'Are you a boy or a girl?' only by the time they are four years old and that children of this age often say that a girl could be a boy if she wanted to, or if she changed her hair or clothes. According to Kohlberg, the child's self-categorization then leads her or him to value same-sex behaviours and to adopt sex-appropriate role-models. These behaviours come to have positive associations and become rewarding in themselves. However, this part of the theory seems more speculative and difficult to test empirically. Although Kohlberg's is not strictly a socialisation account, it does argue that gender identity is acquired and not innate. Like socialisation accounts, it also appears to accept the fact of gender categories and divisions, and asks only how new individuals come to adopt them.

### Sex-differentiated responses to girls and boys

People sometimes feel bound to accept biological accounts of gender because of the way that gender differences emerge so strikingly and so early in life, often despite the desires and hopes of parents. However, a good deal of research, mostly conducted in the 1960s and 1970s, suggests that gender socialisation begins at birth (if not before). The very first question asked of the parents of a newborn child is 'Is it a boy or a girl?' For what possible reasons could we need to know? The question signals that our anticipations and expectations of the child are structured by gender. Without knowledge of the child's gender status we find it less easy to behave appropriately, to say the right things to the parents and siblings. This is an example of what Bem (1993) calls 'gender polarization', one of the three 'lenses of gender' that she says we look through when we perceive our social world.

We may think that we have the same expectations of girls and boys and treat them identically, but research studies suggest that our behaviour toward them differs in subtle ways of which we might be unaware. Walum (1977) (cited in Giddens, 1989) reports a study which used tape recordings of dialogue between grandparents in a maternity ward. The baby was discussed in very different terms depending upon its sex. For example, a boy's cry was interpreted as 'exercising his lungs', whereas in a baby girl it was seen as a sign that help was needed. Parents of newborn children have been found to respond differently to their child depending on its sex. Moss (1967) found that mothers of baby boys stimulated and held their babies more than mothers of girls, who tended to imitate their daughters' vocalisations more than mothers of sons. In another study, Will *et al.* (1976) gave young mothers a six-month-old baby to hold and play with for a short time, and their behaviour was observed. For half of the mothers the baby wore a pink dress and was introduced as Beth. For the other half of the mothers, baby Adam was dressed in blue over-alls. As Beth the baby was smiled at more, was more often offered a doll to play with, and was described as 'sweet' and having a 'soft cry'. Newson *et al.* (1978), in their famous study of child-rearing in Nottingham, found that the mothers in their study were concerned that their children should display gender appropriate characteristics, particularly for boys. Parents' (and others') assumptions about and expectations of female and male children are communicated to them from very early in their lives, and these expectations may become a self-fulfilling prophecy.

### Social learning theory

Although the concept of socialisation does not specify exactly *how* appropriate behaviour is acquired, it is commonly assumed that this happens largely through **reinforcement** (learning), and through **modelling**. Gender-appropriate behaviour is often either directly or indirectly rewarded by parents, teachers and peers. Choices of toys, dress, games and so on are subject to the direct or subtle communication of approval or disapproval from significant others. Interestingly, censure for sex-inappropriate behaviour is likely to be greater for boys than for girls, and girls are more likely to play with both sex-appropriate and sex-inappropriate toys than are boys. It is generally considered worse for a boy to be seen as a sissy than a girl a tomboy, indicating the generally lower value attached (by both sexes) to traditionally feminine attributes.

However it is social learning theory which has been most widely applied in socialisation accounts (Mischel, 1966). Social learning theory relies upon imitation, modelling and vicarious reinforcement to explain the acquisition of gender roles. This argues that by observing others performing gender-appropriate behaviour and being rewarded by approval for doing so, children come to try out the behaviour for themselves and experience its rewards at first hand. Research evidence offers some support for this view, and suggests that nurturant and powerful models (such as parents or teachers) are most likely to be imitated.

Discrete behaviours are learned in this way, but by regularly associating these with the category labels 'girl' and 'boy', children come to develop the idea that there are whole realms of behaviour seen as appropriate to their sex. In addition to real-life models, children have available to them a rich source of symbolic models in television programmes, advertisements, films, books, comics and so on. There has been no shortage of research showing the stereotypical way that females and males are portrayed in these (see Chapter 5). Most studies show that male characters in books and on television greatly outnumber female characters, are portrayed as more active, and that both males and females are depicted in traditional activities and roles. However, most of the research in this area is now quite old, and new research is needed to find out whether there have been significant changes in recent years. More recent research which has attempted to examine children's responses to non-traditional versions of fairy tales (e.g. Davies and Harré, 1990) suggests that children may find them confusing and fail to recognise the atypical female and male roles that are being offered in these stories. The role of the media is examined in more detail in Chapter 5.

It is generally accepted that **learning theory** and social learning theory can account for at least some of the acquisition of gender roles. However, there is some doubt that they can adequately account for the strength of gender identity and its resistance to change. Learning theories cope best when they are explaining the acquisition of specific behaviours, but do less well when trying to account for differences in emotions, desires and motivations, all of which are a crucial part of what it means to be a woman or a man.

### The role of life experiences: moral development

Although it deals specifically with one particular area of development (moral thinking), Carol Gilligan's (1982) account of gender differences gives a more general insight into how women and men may come to be different kinds of people. Gilligan draws on the psychodynamic theory of Nancy Chodorow (see Chapter 4) and, like her, argues that gender differences in personality are rooted in the different kinds of lives that women and men lead in the public and private spheres.

Gilligan's research aimed to challenge Kohlberg's (1969) conception of female moral development as inferior to that of males (see Chapter 1). She argued that one of the reasons why girls sometimes did not perform well on his moral dilemmas was that the issues they raised were not very relevant to women's experience, and that women found these artificial dilemmas difficult to assess because they often felt they needed more details about the particular case before they could make up their minds about appropriate moral action (this 'lack of principle' was one of the reasons they scored badly on the tests). Gilligan therefore decided to study examples of women's moral reasoning in actual decisions they had made regarding an issue of direct relevance to them – whether to have an abortion. From her interview material, Gilligan concluded that women's moral reasoning is quite as sophisticated as that of men and similarly evolves through stages, but that the form of this reasoning is quite different. The reasons for this difference, she claimed, lay in the different life experiences of women and men.

Women's primary caring role in the family, argues Gilligan, gives them a particular kind of experience. The mother is the person who must ensure that her children are healthy and happy, and must try to provide a relatively harmonious world for her husband to return to in the evening. In her daily life, she must constantly weigh up the demands of husband and children and try to do the best for everyone. She must resolve impossible disputes between children and decide whether one child's need to be noisy is greater than another's need for sleep, and she is successful to the extent that everyone ends up reasonably happy, adequately cared for and above all not hurt or damaged by her or anyone else.

By contrast, a man's daily experience is very different. He is thrust into a hierarchical world where people primarily occupy roles and categories and have clearly defined duties and responsibilities to each other arising from their positions. Men live in a moral order governed by rights and obligations, a world of contracts with people to whom they have no emotional attachment and to whom they owe no special responsibility of care. Their relationships with bank managers, sales representatives and administrative assistants are just not particular in the way that mothers' relationships with their children are.

Drawing on Chodorow (1978), Gilligan argues that men feel themselves to be much more self-contained and separate from other people than do women, and that the public world they have created is consistent with this. Their interpersonal dealings are thus based on a morality of rights, on how to defend yourself against attack or invasion by others. It is a simplistic and legalistic black or white morality operating on agreed rules and principles which is possible to maintain only because men deal with other people as occupiers of roles and not as specific persons.

For women, moral thinking is bound up with the particularities of their family ties and with issues of need and responsibility rather than rights and obligations. Gilligan argues that women's is a morality of care and responsibility, arising from their daily experience in the family. So, when faced with the dilemma of whether to allow one child to be noisy at the expense of the other's rest it makes no sense to ask which child has the greater moral right. The question is rather what action would lead to least harm being done to either child, knowing these particular individuals.

It is therefore possible to see that the different life experiences of women and men may contribute substantially to their development into different kinds of people, and moral thinking may be just one example of this.

### Gender roles

Drawing on the sociological perspective of role theory (see Goffman, 1961), the idea of gender roles explains gender socialisation by a dramaturgical metaphor. Like actors in a play, much of our social behaviour may be seen as originating not in the kind of people we are, but in the role we are currently adopting. Many social roles (such as 'police officer', 'teacher' or 'doctor' have a clear set of expectations attached to them regarding appropriate duties, behaviours, manner of dress, speech and so on, and this is also true of roles which are not linked to occupations, such as 'parent', 'teenager' or 'hospital patient', and of course 'woman' and 'man'. The dramaturgical metaphor invites us to view femininity and masculinity as the performance of a role which involves loosely following a script and stage directions. We must learn our lines, our entrances and exits, the appropriate use of props and so on in order to adequately perform our role.

Role theory is often criticised because it seems to imply that much of our social behaviour is superficial or contrived and constitutes a pretence. In some cases this is certainly true; people sometimes do feel a distance or lack of fit between a role and what they feel to be their real self. But in other cases, like our gender, we usually do not feel that we are pretending or putting on an act. However, I think that this is to misunderstand the complexity of what it means to take on a role. Actors themselves often describe getting into a role not as a matter of cloaking their real self in a fake exterior, but of delving into themselves and coming up with some aspect of their own person which can be fleshed out and elaborated to produce the character they must play. George Kelly, the originator of personal construct psychology (Kelly, 1955), advocated what he called 'fixed role therapy' to help bring about personal change. Here the client is required, for a fixed period of time, to play the role of the person they wish to become, and it demonstrates how our state of mind, attitudes, expectations, in short our outlook on life, may be changed by taking up a different role. Playing a role involves much more than going through the motions.

## Feminist accounts of sexuality and aggression

While liberal feminists have explained inequalities in terms of socialisation and Marxist feminists have focused on the economy, radical feminists have pointed to sexuality and male aggression as the cornerstone of women's oppression. They see biological accounts which normalise coercive male sexuality as serving to mask the way that men secure domination over women through sexual means. The central argument here is that sexual relations, which are arguably the most fundamental of human relations, are almost defined by male domination and female submission. Given this power relation in something so fundamental to human life, it is not surprising that other contexts (such as work and the family) have taken their shape from this domination/submission framework. Heterosexuality, as it has become shaped through relations between the sexes, is seen as the problem here, and this is why some radical feminists advocate separatism or lesbian relationships for women.

The nature of women and their sexuality are seen as taking shape only within the demands of men's sexuality. According to Walby, radical feminism argues that 'The eroticization of dominance and subordination creates gender as we know it' (Walby, 1990: 118). Women's very selves become defined in terms of their (male-oriented) sexuality:

> Male sexuality is political and manipulative – it uses the female body to establish the primacy of male gender. In a sense, the ascendancy of male sexuality is demonstrated in male sexual practice – in the manner in which men typically express their 'rights' over women's bodies. Rape, sexual

harassment, the 'wolf-whistle', pornography, emphasize the generalized sexual power of men in society at large. Thus, rape is not a deviant phenomenon, it is rather one dramatic example of the way in which men use women sexually. Sexuality is the terrain, the domain in which both men and women come to define themselves in terms of a taken-for-granted gender identity. For a girl, this definition begins from the moment she is made aware of the coercive nature of men's sexuality. Her father, her brothers, the boys she plays with at school, the media, the books she reads, her own mother, other women and girls, all somehow appear to assent to the passivity of women.

(Brittan and Maynard, 1984: 93–94)

Pornography, rape and sexual harassment thus are not expressions of a natural (and healthy) male sexuality but are statements about and expressions of men's control over women's sexuality, their bodies, and by extension their lives. Radical feminists roundly attack the notion that rape is simply a sexual offence springing from men's natural need for plentiful sex, and argue that the motives for such attacks are overwhelmingly for the purposes of establishing power and control. Susan Brownmiller has developed this idea and argues that rape is 'nothing more or less than a conscious process of intimidation by which *all men* keep *all women* in a state of fear [italics in original]' (Brownmiller, 1975: 15). She believes that through the constant threat of rape (from men in general), women are strongly encouraged to confine themselves to the domestic sphere, under the protection of one particular man (through marriage), who thus reserves his wife's sexual services for himself. It was radical feminism which coined the phrase 'the personal is political', to emphasise the point that the most intimate, personal relations between men and women could not be considered to be unrelated to women's political struggles, which were usually seen as taking place within the public realm of paid work.

## Summary

In this chapter I have summarised the findings of the sex differences research, and looked at some of the problems in interpreting them. Evidence from both research and our everyday experience suggests that women and men do differ in some ways, and I have spent most of the chapter looking at the way that these differences are usually framed in academic debate within psychology, i.e. as a nature–nurture issue. I have described a number of biological arguments which have focused on the role of hormones, brain structure, genes and evolution, and have raised some concerns about the political and ideological uses of such arguments. However, I have also argued that we need to develop theories which look at the role of biology in gender without recourse to essentialist, reductionist and determinist ideas. In examining the nurture side of the debate I have examined the role of socialisation. I have described a number of approaches that attempt to demonstrate how gender might be acquired, through the transmission of expectations, through reinforcement and modelling and through the enactment of accepted gender roles. Liberal feminists often base their arguments on socialisation accounts, and try to raise consciousness about child-rearing practices, educational materials and so on, and aim to change public attitudes toward gender roles. Radical feminists, on the other hand, see gender differences as based in heterosexual relations and regard normal male sexuality and aggression as central to men's domination of women in both the private and public spheres.

## Further reading

Archer, J. and Lloyd, B.B. (1981) 'Problems and issues in research on gender differences', *Current Psychological Reviews*, 1: 287–304. A critical evaluation of sex differences research.

Edley, N. and Wetherell, M. (1995) *Men in Perspective: Practice, Power and Identity*, Hemel Hempstead: Prentice Hall/Harvester Wheatsheaf. This is a good, up-to-date book which, although it focuses primarily upon men, covers a number of approaches to gender, including sociological and feminist accounts.

Fausto-Sterling, A. (1985) *Myths of Gender: Biological Theories about Women and Men*, New York: Basic Books. A clear account and critique of a variety of biological theories of gender.

Hargreaves, D.J. and Colley, A.M. (eds) (1986) *The Psychology of Sex Roles*, London: Harper Row. A collection of chapters by different authors dealing with theories of sex-role acquisition.

Segal, L. (1990) *Slow Motion: Changing Masculinities, Changing Men*, New Brunswick, N.J.: Rutgers University Press. An analysis of the nature of masculinity and its relationship with sexuality.

Chapter 3

# Education

## Gender differences in educational attainment

Until quite recently, gender patterns in educational achievement showed a marked change from primary to secondary school years. Typically, girls' overall performance was greater than boys at primary level, and it is worth pointing out that when IQ tests for children were developed, they were 'standardised' by altering the scales to bring boys' scores up to the level of girls' scores. However, girls' performance at secondary level left them lagging behind the boys. Today girls still do better than boys at primary level, and in terms of overall academic achievement at secondary level they have caught up with boys and have even begun to over-take them, giving rise to widespread media publicity voicing worries about boys' relative under-achievement. A 1993 OFSTED report of National Curriculum assessments of 7-year-olds (key stage 1) in 1991 and 1992 showed girls out-performing boys in reading, spelling and writing. According to the 1993 Department for Education (DFE) Statistical Bulletin, in 1982 roughly equal numbers of girls and boys in England obtained five or more higher grade GCSE or O level passes, but in 1992 more girls than boys did so. In all of the 10 GCSE subjects listed in this docu-ment, with the exception of mathematics, girls achieved higher grades than boys in 1992. In the same year, 28 per cent of girls obtained passes at A level, compared to 23.6 per cent of boys. Girls are therefore no longer lagging behind in terms of overall attainment. The reasons for this reversed trend are not clear, and suggestions that, say, it is because girls mature earlier, or that the style of the new GCSE examinations is better suited to girls' abilities, are purely speculative (reported in *The Sunday Times*, 22 May 1994).

However, if we look beyond overall achievement levels to achievement in specific subjects, the picture becomes more complicated. The relative proportions of girls and boys attempting a modern language at GCSE were 84 per cent and 64 per cent respectively, while over twice as many boys as girls attempted physics, and nearly four times as many boys as girls attempted technology, although in all subjects except maths and sciences more girls than boys obtained higher grades. At A level, over twice as many girls as boys gained passes in English and French, while the position is the reverse for maths, physics and technology.

In higher education, there is a similar story. As a proportion of the population as a whole, men are more likely than women to hold a degree or equivalent qualification, although the gap is narrower among younger people. There has also been a huge increase in the number of women and men entering further and higher education in recent years, and the number of women doing so has grown more quickly than that of men. However, men are more likely than women to obtain a first class degree (they are also more likely to obtain a third class degree), and this has led to worries about possible biases in marking student assessments (Archer, 1992). Subject choices are gendered along traditional lines here also, with men predominating in mathematics, sciences, architecture, engineering and technology, and women predominating in languages, social sciences, education and the arts. In the Netherlands, a government initiative to encourage girls to take natural sciences and mathematics rather than history and languages has had only limited success, and, as elsewhere, subjects like psychology are becoming increasingly female-dominated (Beenen, 1997, personal communication).

The Sex Discrimination Act (1975) made it illegal for schools to discriminate between girls and boys by offering some subjects to only one sex, but this has clearly had little impact upon the traditional pattern of subjects taken.

Curriculum changes have fundamentally restructured teaching in schools in recent years. The advent of the national curriculum is thought by some to ensure that girls and boys receive the same education, although others (Miles and Middleton, 1990;

Mac an Ghaill, 1994) are more sceptical about its benefits, arguing that the absence of flexibility in the curriculum means fewer opportunities for teachers to orient their lessons toward the particular interests and experiences of girls and minority groups.

The gendered pattern of subject choice in both secondary and higher education is of concern, since qualifications in the traditionally masculine areas of science, engineering, and information technology provide routes to the better paid, higher status jobs and careers. First destinations for graduates in the UK (DFE, 1993) showed men going into the better paid jobs in industry and commerce, and women entering relatively lower status work in the public services and education. Although the study of gendered subject choice and achievement has largely focused upon the possible disadvantages to girls and women, some commentators have raised concern about the implications for men. Boys' greater difficulty in subjects like English may be seen as part of a more general difficulty concerning expressing and articulating one's thoughts and feelings, and in communication and social skills. In this respect, the demands of the masculine stereotype may interfere with boys' educational and social development.

## The hidden curriculum

There have been a number of approaches to explaining the differences in educational attainment between girls and boys, and several of these focus upon the way that the school itself may produce and reproduce gender. The mechanisms at work here are usually not thought to be explicit and intentional (although they may be) and are more often thought to operate through subtle processes of which we may be somewhat unaware. A good deal of research into various aspects of gendered schooling was carried out in the 1970s and 1980s, but since that time relatively little research seems to have been published, and there is now a need to find out whether there have been any significant changes in the phenomena that were observed ten or fifteen years ago.

### Who does the teaching?

There is a marked gender imbalance in the number of women and men working as teachers in education and in the posts they hold, and this is a pattern which is not limited to the UK. This imbalance means that girls who might otherwise aspire to high status positions such as head teacher or university professor have relatively few role models available to them. Teaching has traditionally been seen as a suitable occupation for women, and it is no surprise that women teachers far outnumber their male colleagues. Women teachers are concentrated in the nursery and primary sectors, and this may be seen as part of the general feminisation of these in terms of their child-centredness and caring orientation, compared with the focus upon the more impersonal, specialist knowledge of the secondary school. However, although there were twice as many female as male teachers in schools in England and Wales in 1993 (DFE statistics), there were roughly equal numbers of male and female head teachers in nursery/primary education (unfortunately the statistics do not give separate figures for nursery and for primary education), and in secondary education there were over three times as many male as female head teachers. This means that a man entering the teaching profession has a greater chance than his female counterpart of obtaining higher grade teaching posts. One contributing factor in this pattern is that women teachers who temporarily leave teaching in order to care for young children often have difficulty finding teaching jobs later, since they are more expensive to employ than younger teachers with less experience. The gender bias in higher education is also very marked, with university lecturers being predominantly male and female staff having a disproportionately lower chance of being appointed to senior positions.

### Teaching materials

Studies of the materials used in schools, especially reading schemes and text books, have reported that they typically contain stereotypical images of women and men, that women are less visible in these materials, and that the content is oriented toward male interests. In her classic study, Lobban (1975) subjected a number of children's reading schemes to a content analysis and found that they represented males and females in traditional roles and activities, and that they contained many more male than female characters. From a social learning theory perspective, reading schemes and stories often have a clear moral message and implicitly invite children to identify with and model their behaviour on the characters in them. In this way such books are thought to steer children along traditionally sex-typed routes in their development.

The stereotypical images presented endorse and reinforce those found in TV, advertising and comics, etc., and present children with a vision of the world which is not only questionable from the point of view of influencing gender expectations but is also in major respects inaccurate. For example, households are typically represented as consisting of white, heterosexual married parents and their children. If children's books were to accurately reflect contemporary society, many more of them would have to feature single and divorced people, lone parents, families from different ethnic groups and gay couples. Although some schools have gradually replaced their old reading schemes with alternatives that show an awareness of gender and ethnicity issues, we can expect that many schools will not have had the resources available to do this.

Like children's stories and reading schemes, science textbooks are more likely to feature men than women, who are again represented by stereotypical images (Kelly, 1985). According to Mahoney (1985) this can be seen as part of a more general 'trivialisation' of women found in the curriculum. Mahoney describes a science textbook featuring a picture of Marie Curie with her hand on the shoulder of her husband, who is looking down a microscope (Marie Curie, a Polish scientist, was famous for her investigations into radioactivity. She and her husband, Pierre, discovered radium.) Mahoney argues that apart from trivialising women's contribution to science in this way, their contribution in many other areas is marginalised by books and curricula focusing on the achievements of men. Likewise, Spender (a feminist and sociolinguist) argues that text books assume that 'people' are men and focus upon male experience and activities, rendering women invisible:

> When students come to learn about economics or sociology (or language, literature, education, psychology, philosophy, political science, anthropology, science) they are taught about men, and men's view of the world, and this is a lesson in male supremacy.
>
> (Spender, 1982: 27)

Scott (1988) looked at the role of women as depicted in a variety of school textbooks. She also found that the books tended to focus on the activities and achievements of men and to portray women in a subordinate role, and Swann (1992) reports several studies with similar findings. This marginalisation and trivialisation of women and their achievements is thought to influence children's expectations, so that for both girls and boys it really is a man's world and in particular, areas such as science come to be seen by them as a male preserve.

### School organisation and practices

Although the Sex Discrimination Act rules that the same range of subject choices be available to girls and boys, in practice this may not happen due to timetabling decisions. For example, a decision to timetable child development at the same time as technology may be a logical response to student interest but nevertheless helps to reproduce traditionally gendered subject choices. In physical education, girls and boys are still offered different team sports, with football, rugby or cricket for boys and netball or hockey for girls. Teams are very likely to consist of either girls or boys (but not a mix) despite considerable overlap in the physical size and strength of the two sexes during childhood, and school sports days frequently feature separate events for girls and boys.

The message being driven home to children here is one of difference. Gender is seen as sufficient in itself as a reason to separate children's activities, and this message of difference is reinforced by practices such as assigning different tasks to girls and boys (for example, boys may be asked to move furniture and girls to clean equipment), and insisting on different items of school uniform (blouses and skirts for girls, shirts and trousers for boys). Some of the more easily remedied forms of gender differentiation in schools such as recording children's names in the register by sex or getting them to line up as girls and boys may be disappearing, although Woods (1990) reports such practices still in use. Other changes such as assigning non-traditional tasks to each sex may be more difficult to put into effect because they require more conscious effort on the part of teachers and may well be met with some resistance by children themselves, who very early in life acquire an in-depth understanding of what is considered appropriate behaviour for their sex (see Chapter 2).

### Teachers' attitudes and expectations

Teachers at both primary and secondary levels appear to hold different attitudes toward and expectations of their female and male pupils. In studies by Clarricoates (1978, 1980) primary school teachers reported that, although they found the boys harder to control, they felt that they were their most rewarding pupils and preferred to teach them. Even though the boys often did not perform as well in class as the girls, they were generally perceived as brighter and more capable and girls' success tended to be seen as due to hard work rather than ability. Walkerdine (1993) found that teachers tended to explain girls' success in mathematics as due to hard work rather than intelligence, but that boys who did not perform well were nevertheless seen as bright and their lack of achievement was seen as due to other factors, such as disruptiveness. When girls struggle with 'male' subjects like mathematics, teachers are likely to tell them not to worry rather than encourage them to do better, communicating the idea that the teacher doesn't really expect them to be competent in this area. Boys and girls are differentially rewarded and reprimanded, such that boys' work is rewarded and their behaviour or appearance reprimanded, and vice versa for girls. The message being communicated to girls is that they are 'good at' being neat and tidy but academically weak.

Stanworth (1983) conducted interviews with teachers and students at a sixth form college, and reports that the female students in her study felt that they were considered mediocre by their teachers and had internalised this in their own estimations of themselves. She asked teachers to rank their students' academic success and then asked the students themselves to rank that of themselves and their classmates. Compared to teachers' rankings, girls frequently underestimated and boys overestimated their own success, and overall both sexes ranked the boys' success as greater than the girls'.

The interviews with teachers also indicated that they more readily identified their male students and became more attached to them, regardless of academic record. Both male and female students said that their teachers were more concerned about the boys, that the boys were considered to be more capable, and that teachers found them easier to get on with. Teachers' greater concern and liking for the boys and their higher expectations of them are manifested in their tendency to ask them more questions in class and to direct their comments to them.

Gender differences in estimations of ability persist into higher education. Beloff (1992) reports that female psychology undergraduates' average estimations of their own IQ was significantly lower than that of males and that both sexes perceived their intelligence level as similar to that of their same-sex parent, with mothers' IQ being consistently given lower estimations than that of fathers. In terms of academic success, male students are more likely to obtain first and third class degrees than women, who are more clustered around the middle range.

Not only does research suggest that teachers may be raising boys' expectations of themselves and lowering that of girls, but teachers' expectations of the future careers of their pupils reinforces the message. In Stanworth's study, male teachers in particular were either vague about the possible futures of their female students or saw them in domestic roles or occupying stereotypical jobs such as secretarial work or nursing, regardless of the girls' own aspirations. Spear (1985) investigated secondary school teachers' attitudes towards technology as a subject for their pupils to study. The teachers rated it as more important for boys' education than girls' and as more important for boys' future lives. Science teachers also completed a questionnaire to measure their attitudes toward women's roles, and frequently expressed the views that women are not as good as men at complicated technical matters and that their careers are less important than those of men. A sizeable minority felt that women's primary role is the care of their husbands and children. Spear concludes that teachers are likely to convey their attitudes and expectations to their pupils, with the outcome that girls will reject technology and thus restrict their future prospects.

In a large scale study of teachers' attitudes toward equal opportunities issues, Pratt (1985) found that although the majority of teachers (nearly 60 per cent) were sympathetic, many teachers (particularly men) were not. Pratt concluded that even when teachers seem sympathetic in principle, this may not translate into action in terms of developing teaching practices which might encourage equality, and that the reluctance of pupils to take up non-traditional subjects is unlikely to be seen as a problem by many teachers. Mac an Ghaill (1994) found that, in the context of widespread male unemployment, new vocational courses in subjects like technology and business are seen by many (male) teachers as particularly appropriate to the needs and desires of male pupils. In line with other research studies, he also found that some teachers make explicitly sexist remarks to their pupils. For example, teachers may imply that girls in a biology class would feel ill while performing a dissection, that boys who are 'being silly' are acting like girls, or that boys should feel ashamed at being 'beaten' by girls who achieve higher marks than them. Askew and Ross (1988) found a 'common culture' of maleness being played out between male teachers and male pupils, from which both female pupils and teachers were excluded.

In their now famous study, Rosenthal and Jacobson (1968) found evidence to suggest that teachers' expectations of their pupils can become self-fulfilling prophesies. The authors conducted their study in an elementary school in the USA. All the children in a particular class were given a standard IQ test. However, the teacher was told that the test was able to predict which children would show a spurt in intellectual development in the near future. They then randomly selected twenty children from the class and told the teacher that these children could be expected to show such intellectual growth. Eight months later all the children were again tested, and it was found that the children identified showed significantly greater gains in IQ than the other children. Rosenthal and Jacobson concluded that the teacher's expectations toward these children had been communicated to them through her behaviour, producing an actual increase in IQ test performance. Although this particular study has since been criticised on methodological grounds, other similar studies seem to suggest that the general conclusion is still sound. It therefore seems reasonable to assume that the gendered expectations that teachers may hold about their students' abilities and future lives are transmitted to and internalised by them.

## Interaction in the school

### Teacher–pupil interaction

The above analysis seems to suggest that gender differences in education may be due to inappropriate teacher attitudes and expectations. However, although these may indeed play a part in forming pupils' own expectations, as we shall see there are complex interactions taking place in the classroom which cannot be represented as simply the responsibility of teachers.

Observation studies of teachers and pupils interacting within the classroom have identified a number of ways in which this interaction is gendered. One finding that has been reported in a number of studies is that teachers give more attention to their male pupils and spend a greater proportion of their time in interaction with them. Spender (1982) videotaped lessons (including her own) in a secondary school. A conscious decision was made to try to spend as much time with the girls as the boys, and

Spender reports that she sometimes felt that she had overcompensated. However, on analysing the tapes from ten of her lessons she found that she had on average given the girls 38 per cent of her time, and this pattern was similar with other teachers. She says:

> Because we take it so much for granted that boys are more important and deserve more of our time and attention, giving the girls 35 per cent of our time can feel as if we are being unfair to the boys.
>
> (Spender, 1983: 56)

The other teachers were also surprised by the results, and often reported that both they and the boys in their class felt that the teacher had given the girls too much of their attention.

French (1986) used video recordings of interactions in infant classrooms. Although she found, like Spender, that the lion's share of the teacher's time and attention was given to the boys, her observations revealed the way that the children's behaviour helped to produce this pattern. The boys were more disruptive, so that the teacher was often busy trying to keep their attention and control their behaviour, and they called out to or corrected the teacher. By contrast, the girls, who sat quietly in their places and got on with their work, demanded and received less of the teacher's attention. Although interested and keen, they were more likely to follow the rule of handraising and waited for permission to speak. In a detailed analysis of classroom interaction, French and French (1993) showed how some boys were able to monopolise class interaction time with the teacher, for example by answering questions in a way that they knew would elicit a further enquiry from the teacher. The common infant school practice of seating the children on the floor in front of the teacher's chair for a discussion or story was also found to contribute to the overall pattern. Typically, the girls would gather at the front or centre, close to the teacher, and the boys would occupy the margins or periphery. The physical vantage point of the teacher means that she may literally overlook the girls, and, with her focus falling naturally on the boys, direct more of her questions to them.

Gendered patterns of classroom interaction are therefore not in any simple way the fault of teachers, and Trowler (1995) reports research which suggests that this is also true in the secondary school. For example, while it may be true that teachers may orient their science lessons primarily toward the boys in the class, the girls also subtly communicate their distance from the subject by arriving late, avoiding questions and discussion, and finding legitimate excuses that allow them to stop work and chat to other pupils.

### Interaction between pupils

One of the most enduring observations of children's use of playground space is that this is markedly structured by gender. Typically, groups of boys are observed to occupy and monopolise the playground area through games of football or other activities involving running, chasing and physical contact. Whether by intention or by default, this has the effect of consigning the girls, who typically are found in smaller groups or pairs, to the periphery of the playground where they may observe or simply avoid getting in the way of the boys' activity. As Thorne (1993: 83) says, 'In addition to taking up more space, boys more often see girls and their activities as interruptable; boys invade and disrupt all-female games and scenes of play much more often than vice-versa.' Apart from perhaps restricting the girls' use of playground space, the point which researchers have been keen to emphasise is that the boys' monopolising of space is an important 'message' (both to girls and to other boys) that this is *their* territory.

This 'occupation of space' can be seen in a somewhat different guise in the secondary classroom. In her interviews with girls in a secondary school, Mahoney (1985) found that the boys were felt to communicate their ownership of school space by their behaviour. This was true with respect to not only physical space, but also what might be called linguistic space. Girls reported that the boys seemed to intentionally take up space by leaning back in their chairs and spreading themselves out, restricting other's movement. However they also reported that the boys subtly communicated their 'ownership' of linguistic space during lessons. If one of the girls asked a question, the boys would fidget, tap their pencils impatiently, groan and sigh or ridicule them in some other ways and, not surprisingly, girls often said that they preferred not to participate in class discussions. This control of linguistic space is in line with numerous research studies which report that, in cross-sex conversations, men talk for a greater proportion of the time, interrupt more and control the topics of conversation (Anderson, 1988). Some writers argue that differences in conversational style between women and men are not strictly gender differences but are found in any interactions where the status and power of the participants is not matched.

However, not all boys behave in this way, many girls either retaliate or ignore the behaviour, and the requirements of appearing cool and of playing down one's academic ability are very real pressures for both sexes. In addition, it is not only the boys who appear to control the girls' behaviour. Some of the girls in Mahoney's study were unsympathetic to those who regularly chose to risk being put down by the boys, obviously regarding them as having overstepped acceptable boundaries. The problem appears to be less pronounced at primary and early secondary levels, suggesting that emerging developmental and interpersonal issues play a significant role as the pupils reach adolescence. Both the older and the more recent research reported above identifies sexuality and the struggle to achieve and maintain sexual identities as major factors operating in the secondary school. An enormous task facing all adolescents is how to achieve and act out a credible masculine or feminine identity and how to manage their sexuality.

The research suggests that the struggle to achieve a gender and sexual identity is constantly being played out in the school context. For the boys, a traditional masculinity is available through their engagement with other boys in rough physical play or fighting, and through laddish banter (which often includes sexual comments about the girls). Such scenes of masculine activity are acted out not only for the benefit of the girls, but also as a way of establishing boys' masculine status in each other's eyes. According to Abraham (1995), through treating the girls as sexual objects and other forms of sexual harassment, the boys not only create a traditional sexual identity but also create their sense of masculinity as they psychologically distance themselves from the girls and from femininity. In this respect, the study echoes the findings of the earlier classic work by sociologist Paul Willis (1977). Although his primary concern was class (specifically, the relationship between the school subculture of working class boys and their entry into lower status jobs), Willis notes the importance for 'the lads' of macho, sexist and racist behaviour in their struggles to demonstrate their masculinity.

For the girls' part, their struggle for a feminine identity is characterised by conflicts between femininity, sexuality and academic pursuits. Firstly, their sexual reputation is still a major issue for young girls today, who, like the boys, operate a distinction between 'good girls' and 'slags'. The policing and control of the girls' sexuality is therefore not only carried out through sexual harassment from the boys, but also by the girls' own comments about each other. Secondly, traditional femininity is somewhat at odds with intellectual activity. For centuries of western thinking, reason, logic, culture and science have been aligned with masculinity (and have been the province of men) with un-reason, intuition, emotion and nature being the markers of femininity.

Girls are thus faced with the problem of how to become intellectual achievers, especially in areas particularly thought of as masculine, such as science and technology, while living out a credibly feminine identity. Given their additional sexualisation (by both boys and girls) in the school, the girls may be encouraged to develop identities which do not fit well with some kinds of academic achievement. Salmon (1995: 65), drawing upon personal construct psychology, points out that academic performance may have less to do with intelligence or 'natural' abilities than with the difficulties involved in 'stepping right outside our own established identity, into conduct in which we feel ourselves to be unrecognizable'. Women teachers, too, are often faced with a difficult task in marrying their femininity with academic and professional credibility. Askew and Ross (1988), focusing primarily upon boys in single-sex schools, report that women teachers routinely face sexual harassment from their male pupils, who regard them as 'soft' and who are less likely to take them seriously. Women teachers also report that their male colleagues undermine their authority in front of the boys in a variety of ways, and that their male colleagues can also be a source of sexual harassment as well as tending to implicitly condone the harassment they suffer from their male pupils.

Nevertheless, this is not to say that girls and boys have no room for manoeuvre. Gender inevitably interacts in complex ways with other features of school life and its subcultures to provide opportunities as well as limitations for both sexes. For example, in his research in a comprehensive school, Abraham (1995) found a number of different school sub-cultures offering different kinds of identities for their members. In particular, an anti-school group which called themselves 'gothic punks' comprised both male and female pupils and offered non-traditional gender identities for both sexes.

### Gender, race and class

It would be misleading to give the impression that gender is the only source of inequality or oppression in education, or that it operates in isolation from other social and cultural factors. The picture is complicated by the way in which gender interacts with race and class, and although a detailed analysis of this interaction is beyond the scope of this chapter it is appropriate here to give some indication of the nature of this. Black and Asian children of both sexes may experience implicit or explicit racism in their school lives, often in the form of harassment both from other pupils and from teachers so that for some girls racism may be more prominent in their school experience than sexism. Swann (1992) reports studies which suggest that Afro-Caribbean pupils of both sexes receive considerable negative teacher attention, and that in particular Afro-Caribbean girls are seen by teachers as not conforming to conventions of good behaviour. The gap in educational attainment between Afro-Caribbean girls and boys is growing, and it seems likely that cultural differences in gender expectations may play a part in this.

Likewise, class interacts with gender so that differences in educational experiences between girls and boys are not simple. For example, Grafton *et al.* (1987) show how working class girls are channelled into subject choices which prepare them for domesticity rather than intellectual pursuits. The picture that is emerging is that the gendering of education is a complex phenomenon that cannot be simply reduced to the behaviours or attitudes of individual teachers. The school is a complex micro-society whose practices and assumptions cannot be studied in isolation from the wider society of which it is a part.

## Strategies for change

### *Single-sex teaching environments*

Some commentators have pointed out that girls in single-sex schools often do better than those in coeducational schools. It is argued that in these schools girls are not subject to representations of sexuality and femininity to the same extent as girls who are educated alongside boys, that there is less gendering of activities and that they have available to them more female role models in high status positions such as head teacher or head of department and in 'male' subjects such as maths and sciences.

However, it is difficult to evaluate this claim, since a straightforward comparison between single-sex schools and coeducational schools cannot be made. Single-sex schools are a minority, and many of them are operating outside the comprehensive system as grammar schools or are privately funded. This means that their pupils will be drawn from predominantly middle class families and that any comparison of achievement levels with coeducational comprehensive schools would therefore be confounded with the issue of class.

Some coeducational schools have introduced experimental teaching methods whereby girls and boys are taught separately for some lessons. One intervention reported by Deem (1984), carried out over a period of two years, involved teaching mathematics and science in single-sex sets and showed that girls' achievement in these subjects improved. Single-sex teaching has sometimes been adopted as part of broader intervention projects of the kind outlined below.

### 'Action research' projects

Occasionally, funding has been given to research into gender inequalities in education which involves coordinating interventions across a number of schools. The first of these was GIST (Girls Into Science and Technology), and involved a number of coeducational comprehensive schools in Manchester (UK). GIST aimed to improve girls' attitudes to the physical sciences and technical subjects. The intervention consisted of raising gender awareness among the teachers and encouraging them to introduce interventions of their own, such as single-sex classes, the development of 'girl-friendly' curriculum materials, and raising gender awareness with the pupils themselves. Although the project was found to be successful in changing the attitudes of the pupils, its impact on subject choices was less than had been hoped. This suggests that subject choices are determined by a variety of influences, only one of which is the attitudes of pupils and teachers. Acker (1994) points out that many of the teachers involved in the project, especially male teachers, did not believe gender inequality in schools to be a problem and were concerned that positive action for girls may discriminate against boys. 'Teacher resistance' may therefore be a problem for initiatives of this kind.

### Encouraging 'good practice'

Individual teachers who are concerned about gender differences and inequalities in their own school have sometimes tried to change policy and practice by getting the other teachers on board and thus achieving coordinated action on gender. This stands a greater chance of success than the limited changes that they can make in their own practice alone. Sometimes schools have been able to obtain funding for their initiatives if their local education authority was sympathetic to equal opportunities issues. Initiatives of this kind might involve changes in the curriculum, in teaching practice, raising awareness in pupils, or developing an equal opportunities policy for the school. However, as with the action research described above, success will depend upon the level of commitment from the staff as a whole and from the head teacher in particular. Guidelines for good practice have been drawn up by the Centre for the Study of Comprehensive Schools.

Despite the concern of some teachers regarding equal opportunities issues, the impact of the national curriculum in the UK has meant less space and opportunity to challenge gender. Teachers have also been required to implement new assessment methods and to cope with rapid changes imposed by the government, all of which has understandably pushed equal opportunities further down their list of priorities. In many areas, high levels of unemployment have meant that the communities served by some schools may be primarily concerned about the lack of jobs for boys leaving education, and schools who push equal opportunities issues in such a climate may well be unpopular.

## Feminist analyses of gender in education

The research findings and interventions described above may now be analysed in terms of the feminist positions outlined in Chapter 1. The research on teachers' attitudes towards and expectations of their pupils suggests that these often run along traditionally gender stereotyped lines. A liberal feminist perspective argues that through our socialisation practices (both in the school and in the home) we are still unthinkingly transmitting sexist attitudes and expectations from one generation to the next, and that these attitudes are instrumental in, for example, the differential careers advice that teachers give to girls and boys and the subject choices that pupils make. Women's disadvantage is thus seen as the regrettable but unintended outcome of prejudiced or irrational beliefs about the sexes, and we should therefore try to change the beliefs that people hold about women and men, perhaps through raising awareness in teacher training or by changing school materials, and the provision of more female role models through the removal of structural barriers and equal opportunities legislation. This is the kind of rationale which is consistent with initiatives like GIST and efforts to establish equal opportunities policies in schools, although of course such initiatives may not be explicitly driven by any particular feminist principles or theory.

Although the educational aims of liberal feminists (changing socialisation practices and attitudes, and legislating for equal educational opportunities for both sexes) are admirable, the approach is criticised by other feminists for failing to acknowledge the role that patriarchy, the labour market and capitalism play in creating inequality. It is argued that liberal feminism has a tendency to 'blame the victim' by concentrating upon the lack of confidence or gendered expectations of girls and that this is a form of psychological reductionism (that is, reducing complex societal forces to the operation of intra-psychic events and processes).

The findings on teacher–pupil and pupil–pupil interaction support a radical feminist perspective. They suggest that boys, through their behaviour (which is in many ways condoned or at least not checked by teaching staff) actively control the girls and limit their participation in school. This behaviour is seen as an example of patriarchy and in essence no different from the numerous ways in which men as a class control women and their access to resources both in the domestic sphere and in paid work. Thus the school is not wholly responsible for gender inequality but plays its part, alongside the other male-dominated institutions, in shoring up patriarchy. It follows that the school can therefore not be solely responsible for the eradication of gender inequality. However, the school must still bear its share of the responsibility and do what it can to make changes. This would involve shifting education from its 'male baseline' (Weiner, 1994) in a variety of ways. This would include an active concern with issues of sexuality in the school, aimed at analysing the ways that masculinity, femininity and sexuality are related to male power (Jones and Mahoney, 1989), and challenging the male-oriented knowledge base of education. Providing single-sex sets for some subjects is consistent with this view, since it acknowledges the way that power relations between girls and boys in the classroom and issues of sexual identity can structure the learning experience. Epstein (1993), although her primary focus is racism, also goes beyond a liberal feminist approach in her painstaking examination of and intervention in interactions in the primary classroom. Not only does she encourage children to reflect upon their own sexist assumptions, but she enables power relations to be challenged by actively engaging the girls and boys in alternative ways of structuring relations between them and getting them to discuss and reflect upon the changes this brings about.

Marxist and socialist feminist (dual systems) theorists are less optimistic about the likelihood of change in education, since they see education as one of the prime sites in which both class and gender inequalities are produced and reproduced for the benefit of capitalism. The education system is therefore itself a key agent of oppression because of the way that, through ideology, it reinforces class and gender divisions while passing itself off as egalitarian. The school supports capitalism by producing large numbers of young women whose abilities and skills are less valued that those of young men, and who thus form a potential 'reserve labour force' of cheap, casual or part-time workers. These theorists therefore see the goal as the elimination of *both* class and gender oppression by the eradication of capitalism and the class system.

## Summary

Although girls are now equalling and even surpassing boys in their overall levels of academic achievement, there is still a marked difference in the GCSE, A level and degree courses which girls and boys choose. These choices remain stereotypically gendered, and it has been argued that girls are disadvantaged by this in the labour market and that boys too may be disadvantaged in terms of social skills and understanding.

Research suggests that this pattern may be the result of a number of social and psychological processes operating within the school. School materials and practices as well as the attitudes and expectations of teachers may all play a part in forming the expectations that pupils have of themselves. Furthermore, the gender imbalance in the teaching profession itself means that female role models occupying higher status positions or teaching gender-atypical subjects are a minority. In addition to these messages, research also suggests that the struggle to achieve a satisfactory masculine or feminine identity during adolescence may make different kinds of academic achievement difficult for each sex. However, research at both primary and secondary level indicates that boys (perhaps non-consciously) regard both physical and educational space as primarily for their own use and, by their behaviour as a group, control girls' participation in educational processes and undermine their confidence, especially in 'male' subjects. Teachers may also explicitly or implicitly condone this by their own comments and behaviour.

Strategies for addressing gender issues in schools have been adopted in some schools in the past, and these have had varying degrees of success. I have discussed the research findings and these strategies in terms of liberal, radical and socialist feminist theories, which differ in the degree to which they see the school as able to address gender inequalities and in their analyses of how change might be brought about, that is, the kinds of interventions they would regard as appropriate or likely to be effective.

## Further reading

Arnot, M. and Weiner, G. (1987) *Gender and the Politics of Schooling*, London: Hutchinson. An excellent collection of chapters, covering a wide range of educational issues.

Askew, S. and Ross, C. (1988) *Boys Don't Cry: Boys and Sexism in Education*, Buckingham: Open University Press. A short but lively and informative book looking at the role of masculinity in producing sexism in education.

Ruddock, J. (1994) *Developing a Gender Policy in Secondary Schools*, Buckingham: Open University Press. Practical advice aimed at teachers, based on research with teachers themselves.

# Work and family

## The gender division of labour

When considering the question of equality between women and men, people often point to the large scale entry of women into the labour force as evidence of change. Women now constitute 45 per cent of the labour force in Britain (EOC, 1996), we have seen a woman become prime minister for the first time in our history and marriage and family life are no longer seen as necessarily preventing a woman from pursuing a career. Nevertheless, there is ample evidence to show that women and men do not enjoy equality in the workplace. There is a gender division of labour which operates both vertically and horizontally.

The 'vertical division of labour' refers to the inequality in status and pay between the sexes. The Equal Pay Act (1970) made it illegal for employers to pay different rates to women and men for the same work. However, women in the UK in full-time work today are paid only 80 per cent of the average hourly rate for men. There are at least two reasons for this. First, when the Act was passed, employers were given a period of five years in which to bring their pay levels into line with it. But in many cases, employers used this time to find ways of defining the work that women did so that they could claim that it was not the same as the work carried out by their male employees. Second, although more women are in paid employment than previously, they are concentrated in lower status (and therefore lower paid) positions. For example, according to the EOC (1996) only 33 per cent of managers and administrators are women, compared to 80 per cent of company secretaries. To complete the picture, it has to be remembered that a great many women who are economically active are not in full-time employment. Nearly half of all employed women are in part-time (and usually lower paid) jobs, compared to less than 10 per cent of employed men. The picture is similar in the USA and in other countries outside of the UK. For example, pre-tax income for women in the Netherlands is approximately 77 per cent of that of men (Beenan, 1997, personal communication) and women in New Zealand earned about 80 per cent of their male counterpart's wages in 1996 (*New Zealand Herald*, 13 June 1997).

The 'horizontal division of labour' refers to the way that jobs and careers are gendered, giving rise to men's jobs and women's jobs. Doctors, computer analysts and programmers, and electrical or electronics engineers are much more likely to be men, whereas nurses, primary and nursery school teachers, clerical and secretarial workers and care assistants are mainly women. Women's jobs thus mirror both women's perceived caring and supportive role in the family and their subject choices at school (see Chapter 3). The horizontal and vertical divisions interact such that, even in careers associated primarily with women (such as teaching, nursing and hairdressing) men entering these professions are likely to secure the higher status positions. In the first few years after leaving school, both sexes have similar rates of employment (about 60 per cent). However, between the ages of twenty and sixty-five men's rate of employment exceeds that of women by about 25 per cent. It seems very likely that this is due to women's greater family responsibilities, and signifies that gendered work roles must be studied alongside family roles.

The explanations for these patterns that psychologists have drawn upon have, not surprisingly, been located at the level of the individual psyche and have treated gender patterns in employment as if they could be understood solely as psychological issues. Gender inequalities in paid work have been explained in terms of women's fear of success or lack of motivation which, apart from ignoring important social factors, also invites us to blame women themselves for their situation. The theories that psychologists have used have tended to be restricted to biological or socialisation models. For example, as I described in Chapter 2, evolutionary accounts argue that, through the mechanisms of natural and sexual selection, women and men have emerged with different psychological dispositions (nurturance and a non-promiscuous sexuality for women, aggressiveness and promiscuity for men). In addition, differences in hormonal action are claimed to lie behind gender differences in spatial and verbal ability. It is supposed that these tendencies account for the greater visibility of men in the world of work (and women's greater involvement in homemaking and childcare), differences in choice of job or career, as well as pay differentials. Here, it is argued that women's lesser aggressiveness and assertiveness prevents them from pushing their way to the top, well-paid jobs. Although biological accounts have enjoyed an increasing degree of attention in recent years, they fail to explain why there are cross-cultural differences in what is considered appropriately men's or women's work and serve to pathologise women and men who do not display sex appropriate behaviour and desires. For example, biological accounts have difficulty in explaining why some women do not wish to become mothers, and such women are still seen by many people as unnatural, sick or selfish. The medical profession has long regarded motherhood as the pinnacle of feminine development, drawing heavily on psychoanalytic theory. The view expressed here is not unusual:

> The very fact that a woman cannot tolerate pregnancy, or is in intense conflict about it, or about giving birth to a child, is an indication that the pre-pregnant personality of this woman was immature and in that sense can be labelled as psychopathological . . . pregnancy and birth are the overt proofs of femininity.
>
> (Fromm, 1967: 210)

Alternatively, socialisation models focus upon the learning experiences to which children are exposed from a very early age, in the family, school and wider culture. Differences in toys, parental expectations, stereotyped images in books and television programmes, etc. have all been identified as potential explanations of gender differences in career aspirations (see Chapter 2 for details). It may be, for example, that boys are more usually given toys which encourage them to develop particularly good spatial skills, such as building blocks and construction kits. Likewise, girls who are given toy domestic appliances and dolls are being handed the opportunity to model themselves on their mother and other women (who are still primarily responsible for household and childcare tasks) and to develop their personal repertoire of caring and domestic behaviours. Also, parents are often intolerant of aggressive and rough behaviour in girls, but are inclined to believe that 'boys will be boys' in this respect, thus allowing the development of aggressive behaviour in boys and curtailing it in girls.

These explanations may go some way to accounting for the gender divisions of labour, but they are somewhat incomplete as they generally fail to take into consideration the wider economic and social conditions within which women's and men's working lives are set. As might be expected, feminist analyses often concentrate on these and offer more sociological accounts of gender divisions. These accounts may well be compatible with socialisation arguments, and therefore provide opportunities to develop theories which do not reduce gender divisions either to psychological mechanisms or structural forces alone. Another good reason for considering feminist analyses is that they often explicitly examine the way that work and family roles interact with each other to produce the gender divisions that we observe. I will therefore now go on to talk about the domestic division of labour, before looking at the explanations on offer for women's position in paid work and their domestic role, and for how these might interact.

### The domestic gender division of labour

Numerous studies carried out over the last twenty years or so have looked at how household and childcare tasks are divided up between women and men in the home. Although in most of the studies the researchers carried out interviews with married couples, they tended to use a variety of different measures so that the results are often not directly comparable with each other. Nevertheless, the overall pattern of results suggests a common theme. Despite the fact that more women are entering paid employment, men's role in domestic labour has changed little.

Conducting research nearly a decade apart, Oakley (1974) and Boulton (1983) looked at samples of middle class and working class fathers, and estimated their contribution to childcare tasks. Their findings were very similar. Although more middle class than working class fathers (around a quarter of them) had a 'high' or 'extensive' contribution, on the whole the majority of fathers' contributions were 'low' or 'minimal'. More accurate measures, using estimates of actual time spent performing tasks, reveal a similar arrangement. Russel (1983) looked at the time spent by mothers and fathers in various childcare tasks, and compared the figures for mothers in paid work with those who were unemployed. Russel found that for couples where the mother was unemployed, mothers spent approximately 51 hours per week in childcare tasks, and fathers spent 13 hours. Where the mother was employed, her time dropped to 25 hours, but fathers' contributions remained the same. Croghan (1991) compared the relative lengths of mothers' and fathers' working days (including both paid and domestic work) using a diary method over a 24 hour period. She found that although fathers worked longer hours in paid employment than their partners (an average of 6.5 hours compared to 0.9 hours), the women's contribution to domestic and childcare tasks (13.2 hours) was much greater than that of the men (1.2 hours) so that their total working day was nearly seven hours longer and nearly double that of fathers.

The pattern with respect to household tasks is similar. In 1993, a survey conducted by the Henley Centre (a forecasting organisation) reported that women spend on average 34 hours per week shopping, cooking and cleaning compared to 13 hours for men. Where both husband and wife are in full-time paid employment, women spent an average of 24 hours per week on household tasks, compared to 14 hours for men. The report concluded that:

> Domestic roles remain surprisingly traditional. Men are helping out more than they used to, but not as much as they or their partners feel they ought to.
>
> (*Independent on Sunday*, 25 July 1993)

Within this overall pattern there seem to be particular tasks which men and women are more likely to perform. Antill and Cotton (1988) in Australia and Horna and Lupri (1987) in Canada showed that women were primarily responsible for cooking, cleaning and childcare and men for household and car maintenance. More recently, the market research organisation Mintel published a report in 1993 which suggests that although men are most likely to contribute to shopping and washing up, women still do most of the shopping, washing up, cooking, cleaning and laundry with men primarily responsible for DIY tasks and gardening. Where childcare tasks are concerned, Russel (1983) and Lewis (1986) both found that fathers' contributions are more likely to be in tasks such as feeding, putting to bed and playing with the child. They are less likely to be involved in bathing the child, changing its nappy, preparing its food or attending to it in the night. In addition, Lewis and O'Brien (1987) suggest that fathers' participation in childcare is always seen (by both themselves and their partners) relative to (low) *expectations* and therefore appears subjectively to be greater than it actually is.

The evidence seems to suggest that changes in attitudes are taking place more rapidly than changes in practice. In a US study reported by Hood (1993), male students' attitudes toward women's and men's roles were compared over a ten year period. The more recent views expressed were more liberal in that they were in favour of men and women having the right to choose whether to opt for a career or family life. However, although the men defended women's right to choose, most of them stated that they themselves would not opt for a domestic role in preference to a career. A further study which examined adolescents' expectations of adult roles found that most girls expected to work outside of the home before and after having children and anticipated that their career would be interrupted by childcare responsibilities. While the boys expected that they would be involved in childcare to some extent, they did not expect their careers to be interrupted by this. In a recent review of the literature, Pleck (1993) concludes that men are indeed taking on a greater share of household tasks than previously, but that they have not taken on family roles to the same extent that women have taken on paid work roles. Thus, although both women and men may express egalitarian attitudes regarding work and family roles, in practice the division of labour in the home continues to operate along unequal, traditional lines.

There are several features of this pattern of findings which need to be explained. We need to explain why there is an unequal division of labour in the home, with women working for longer hours in domestic labour at a greater variety of tasks than men, why there is a division of labour in terms of the kinds of domestic and childcare tasks that women and men perform, and why it is that women are primarily responsible for the care of children. Each of the theories described below goes some way towards answering these questions, but none are total explanations.

## Explanations of the domestic division of labour

### 'Equity' and 'exchange' theories

This represents the idea that women and men make different but equitous contributions to the home. Their contributions cannot be said to be *equal*, since they are of different kinds and magnitude, but they are *equitous* in that their contributions can be said to be roughly equivalent to each other. The gender roles of men and women are seen as complementary, with men taking an instrumental role (providing financial support for the family through paid work) and women taking an expressive role (caring for husband and children). These terms are primarily associated with the sociological perspective of functionalism, and in particular with the sociologist Talcott Parsons. For Parsons (Parsons and Bales, 1953), these different gender roles are *functional* for society. The family, as a social institution, performs the essential tasks of socialising children and providing stable adults. Parsons felt that it was neccessary to keep the gender roles separate from each other to avoid conflict and tension between the public, occupational sphere and the private, family sphere, and that the instrumental and expressive roles of men and women were complementary to each other.

The social-psychological theory of exchange is closely linked with **equity theory** and has also been used to understand gender roles. Scanzoni (1970) argued that husbands contribute as bread-winners in exchange for their wives' provision of emotional support and household services. In this view, each partner's contribution creates a psychological obligation on the other to provide their own complementary contribution, creating a continual balance. This theory cannot in principle explain why the divison of labour takes the particular form that it does (the content of gender roles), although this is often overlooked.

The notion of equity clearly works best when applied to a family structure where men are in full-time paid work and their wives are engaged in full-time domestic and childcare duties. Thus it can be argued that, with recent large increases in (especially male) unemployment and the increase in the number of women in paid employment, equity theory explains the domestic division of labour in only some households. As long ago as 1979, Pleck wrote:

> It is simply not intellectually tenable to view men's limited family roles as the result of an equitable 'exchange' between husband and wife resulting from their different resources. The traditional perspective may fit the data for the declining minority of husband-sole-breadwinner families, but it breaks down when applied to the emerging majority of two-earner families.
>
> (Pleck, 1979: 485)

The notion of equity additionally implies consensus – it assumes that the division of labour is negotiated between husbands and wives with respect to their joint interests. Thus it suggests that women choose not to take up paid employment as a result of a jointly agreed 'household work strategy' which works in the inter-ests of both partners. While this may indeed adequately represent the situation in some families, it does not account for the dissat-isfaction with their roles expressed by many people. Many women experience the domestic division of labour as inequitous and struggle to create what they see as a more balanced sharing of responsibilities. Conversely some men, especially middle class men, are becoming increasingly dissatisfied with what they see as unreasonable career demands and sometimes regret the extent to which it excludes them from family life.

Equity and exchange theories may partially explain why women take on the lion's share of domestic and childcare duties, but, in addition to their other problems, cannot explain why some domestic and childcare tasks are performed more readily by men than others. The idea of gender roles, which is the foundation of equity and exchange theories, relies on the notion that some domestic and childcare tasks are more consistent with the masculine or feminine role than others. These roles are based on culturally available prescriptions about what men and women are like (masculinity and femininity) and are internalised by women and men so that they feel natural (although it is usually left unclear as to how this internalisation is achieved). Thus women's caring and homemaking activities and men's career orientation and involvement in heavy or dirty tasks such as DIY, repairs and gardening are the product of gender roles. However, this explanation breaks down when we try to explain why, when men do participate in household and childcare tasks, they perform certain tasks more readily than others.

### Limitations on men's involvement

Another possible explanation for men's lesser involvement in household and childcare tasks is that the structure of men's lives places limitations on what they can do in the home. This does not only mean that, where men are in paid work, they are absent from the home for large periods of time and are therefore simply not available to perform domestic tasks. It also means that they are not in a position to become familiar with all the tasks that have to be done, or with how they are done. Within this view, the best that men can do is to become a helpmate for their partner, performing tasks which require little expertise. Women may therefore come to take on numerous domestic tasks because they have learned how to do them quickly and efficiently and to

involve their partners would be more time-consuming and less effective. However, although this view does go some way to explaining both men's lesser involvement and the difference in tasks performed, it still suffers from the same difficulty as gender role explanations. It becomes implausible to suggest that men opt for doing the shopping rather than the laundry, or for feeding their children rather than changing their nappies either because these tasks are more consistent with the masculine role or because they demand less expertise. The alternative view, outlined in the next section, is that women and men differ in the degree to which they are given a choice in the matter, and that, as rational people, men choose the more appealing tasks.

### Power inequalities

Some writers have explained the inequalities and differences in the domestic gender division of labour in terms of power inequalities in the family. In other words, men do not take on an equal burden of household and childcare tasks because they can choose not to. In addition, when they do participate they can choose to perform the less unpleasant and less demanding tasks. Using interview material, several studies have demonstrated that, regardless of the actual level of participation of men in household and childcare tasks, the overall responsibility for these is seen by both sexes as falling to women and thus men's contribution is construed as 'help' and therefore optional (Boulton, 1983; Lewis, 1986; Backett, 1987).

Interestingly, however, the power imbalance between husbands and wives was usually not articulated by them as such nor was it necessarily represented as problematic. Backett (1987) argues that the emotional attachments between husbands and wives lead them to psychologically invest in accounts of the inequality which do not threaten the relationship. In her research, she found that when couples became aware that there was a discrepancy between their beliefs that they had a fair division of labour and their actual contributions to childcare, they adopted various coping mechanisms:

In the joint interviews, for instance, spouses frequently reassured one another that they *were* adopting the fairest solution in the prevailing circumstances. Such beliefs were further sustained by stressing that the father was (a) *willing* to do things for the children when necessary, (b) *able* to do things for them *if* necessary and (c) *had* demonstrated such voluntarism and ability on previous occasions. This final point is of crucial importance, as such 'practical proof' did not have to be regularly demonstrated, or achieve the same standards as that of the mother, for it to be judged adequate by the couple.

(Backett, 1987: 87–88, italics in original)

Croghan (1991) interviewed mothers about their husbands' lower participation in childcare. She found that mothers drew upon a number of common ideas when accounting for this. As with earlier research, she found that responsibility for childcare was experienced by the mothers as lying with them, and their husbands were seen as opting in to tasks. When accounting for men's lesser involvement, they readily explained this in terms of men's employment commitments, which were also presented as too demanding to justify asking them to do further work in the home during the evening. They also explained it in terms of differences in personality and abilities between the sexes, or in terms of individual personality characteristics. For example, one mother explained that her husband did not get up in the night to attend to the child when it cried because he was a heavy sleeper, while others saw their husbands as ill-equipped to carry out some tasks because they were disorganised, distractable or made too much mess.

Attempts by psychologists to identify psychological factors which might predict greater involvement of fathers in childcare have generaly drawn a blank, or at the most produced equivocal results. According to Lewis (1986) there seems to be no sound evidence that men who have some feminine as well as masculine qualities take a greater interest in childcare, nor that men's own experience of being fathered has any predictable influence. The increasing trend toward fathers being present at the birth of their child led some to speculate that this would strengthen the bond between the father and child and that this in turn would result in greater involvement in childcare. Again, Lewis (1986) reports that research has found no such relationship.

It seems unlikely that the domestic gender division of labour can be explained by purely psychological processes, but that gender roles and expectations as well as personality attributes are bound up with the kinds of lives men and women lead and the power inequalities between them. It it also necessary to point out that power relations never simply operate in one direction, and that for some women the domestic sphere is the arena in which they are in control and their husbands and other family members must defer to them. For this reason it may not always be straight-forwardly in their interests to have their husbands take on more domestic responsibilities, which would to some degree dilute their only source of power. Feminist analyses have, in different ways, tried to explain inequalities in work and how these are related to domestic roles.

## Feminist analyses of women's position in the public and private spheres

### Liberal feminism

For liberal feminists, changes in women's position in paid work and in the family would be brought about through the dual action of legislation and changes in societal attitudes (through educa-tion). Studies of women and work within this theoretical framework tend to focus upon the different values and expecta-tions held by the sexes and the male culture of organisations, but usually do not attempt to place these within a broader structure of material or power relations.

### Marxist feminism

Marxist feminists see capitalism as at the root of women's oppres-sion. With the advent of the industrial revolution, production

87

moved out of the home and into the factory. Prior to the industrial revolution, the home was the economic unit of production. The family would grow its own food, weave cloth, etc., and husband, wife and children would all be involved in this process, and goods or food in excess of the family's own needs could be sold. With the growth of large-scale production in factories, men had to sell their labour to capitalist employers, leaving women at home caring for children and carrying out the reproductive work (cooking, cleaning, rearing children, attending to the family's health needs, etc.) vital to keeping the workforce fit and healthy. In response to this situation, workers campaigned for a family wage, a wage which was to reflect the fact that a man had a wife and family to support at home. Of course, this wage does not equal the value of the labour contributed by the man and his wife, which is why capitalism is seen as exploitative. This family wage, however, ensured lower wages for women who needed to work, since employers could argue that women were already effectively being benefited via their husband's wage. In addition, women now constituted what has been called a 'reserve army of labour', a flexible and cheap secondary labour force that could be employed or laid off according to fluctuations in the economy For example, during the Second World War women were encouraged to work in the munitions factories because of the shortage of men. However after the war, as men returned and needed work, women were encouraged back into the home, and all of this was wrapped up in an enormous amount of propaganda about what a woman's proper role should be, often using ideas from psychology such as 'maternal deprivation' (Bowlby, 1952). Marriage thus became an economic necessity for women, who could not hope to support themselves adequately by paid work alone, ensuring that the reproductive work important to capitalism's success continued to be carried out by women at little cost to employers. This view of women's role in capitalism led some feminists to call for wages for housework. To pay women for the reproductive work that they do would both call attention to capitalism's ideological mode of operation and serve to lessen women's exploitation.

Although Marxist feminism usefully draws attention to the way that women are positioned within capitalism, it is not a wholly adequate account of gender divisions in work. Marxism cannot really explain why it was women (and not men or both sexes) who remained in the home with the advent of paid work. It fails to recognise that gender inequality existed prior to the industrial revolution and it is therefore more likely that:

> the oppression of women, although not a functional pre-requisite of capitalism, has acquired a material basis in the relations of production and reproduction of capitalism today.
>
> (Barrett, 1988: 249)

Also, Marxist feminism fails to recognise that women's domestic labour benefits men (husbands) as well as capitalists (employers). As women are paid less than men they should be more attractive to capitalism as employees, but there is clearly a tension here between capitalism's need for cheap labour and men's need to retain women's services in the home. Nevertheless, the family and women's role within it is recognised as an important factor in women's position in paid work, and the interaction between these is even more important for socialist feminist (dual systems) theorists.

### Socialist feminism

This framework sees both class (employers' control over workers) and patriarchy (men's control over women) as important in understanding women's position in the labour market. Theorists differ in the extent to which they see patriarchy and capitalism as working as independent, parallel systems. Additionally, although the interests of capitalism and patriarchy may some-times be in harmony, many dual systems theorists recognise that they may also pull in opposite directions and Walby (1990) argues that capitalism and patriarchy constitute two rival systems, each drawing women's labour away from the other. However, in general they agree that there is both a class and a gender struggle operating in society which combine to produce women's position in paid work. For example, Heidi Hartmann sees job segregation by sex (the horizontal division of labour) as crucial to a 'vicious circle' which traps women into both marriage and low-paid jobs. Walby (1990) gives a succinct account of Hartmann's view:

> It is by excluding women from the better kinds of paid work that men are able to keep women at a disadvantage. Men are able to do this largely because they are better organized than women. Hartmann draws on examples of men organized in trade unions which excluded women, such as nineteenth-century craft unions, and the support of the state for the exclusion of women from certain forms of paid work. These practices are not new but existed in pre-capitalist times; for instance, the organization of men in guilds in medieval England. When men are in the better paid jobs they are able to marry women on favourable terms, ensuring that wives do the majority of the housework and child care. Women, who need their husbands' financial support, are in no position to refuse. Men's access to the better jobs results in their earning the so-called family wage. Women's domestic work further hinders their ability to gain access to the better forms of work which require training. Thus we see a vicious circle in which women's forced absence from the best jobs leads to their disproportionate domestic burdens, which contributes to their lack of access to the best jobs.
>
> (Walby, 1990: 39–40)

Hartmann thus takes as her starting point men's control over women's access to jobs in the public sphere, but sees this as strengthened by the additional control they exert over women in the private sphere.

Both Marxist and socialist feminists see women's work and family roles as intertwined, although they largely characterise women's consent to their oppression as no more than a material necessity. They fail to explain why women seek intimacy through marriage, why they often feel the desire to bear children and why many of them seem to freely choose to make home and family their primary concern, at least for a time. These psychological issues have, however, been addressed by some feminists. Juliet Mitchell, drawing on Freud, holds that patriarchal relations are deeply embedded in the unconscious and that we therefore cannot expect change to come about either through equal opportunities legislation or changes in socialisation practices. In her view, change will only be brought about by a complete revolution in (patriarchal) human society. Other theorists such as Nancy Chodorow and Shulamith Firestone (see below), address the psychological differences between men and women and locate them within the division of labour by which men occupy the public and women the private sphere.

### Psychoanalytic feminism: Chodorow's account of mothering

This psychological explanation of the domestic division of labour, particularly childcare, attempts to relate personality differences between women and men to their different social roles. Nancy Chodorow, a psychodynamic theorist working in the USA, criticised both existing psychological and sociological explanations of women's primary responsibility for childcare. In her analysis of why it is women who do most of the mothering, rather than this being performed by men or being shared, she first attacks social learning theory. Social learning theory as an explanation for gender roles has not really been formally articulated, but nevertheless has been (rather uncritically) widely accepted by those who wish to take the nurture side of the nature–nurture debate in this issue. It is often claimed that women become mothers because they are reinforced for maternal behaviour both as children and adults, because they imitate the behaviour of their mothers (and are rewarded for doing so), and because they are provided with dolls and other toys which encourage such modelling. While these processes may indeed operate, Chodorow (1978) claims that this does not provide a complete explanation, and she simultaneously attacks the feminist view that women do most of the mothering because men won't do it. Women do not take care of children simply because they are expected to or because men refuse to. She says:

> it is evident that the mothering that women do is not something that can be taught simply by giving a girl dolls or telling her that she *ought* to mother. It is not something that a girl can learn by behavioural imitation, or by deciding that she wants to do what girls do. Nor can men's power over women explain women's mothering ... (Men) cannot require or force her to provide adequate parenting unless she, *to some degree* and *on some unconscious or conscious level*, has the capacity and sense of self as maternal to do so.
>
> (Chodorow, 1979: 33, italics in original)

The final phrase is the key to Chodorow's view. She argues that it is women's sense of self which is radically different from that of men and which propels them into motherhood and childcare. However, this sense of self does not have biological origins but is a product of the particular social structure and family form that is prevalent in western industrialised societies.

Chodorow takes as her starting point the public/private divide, with men primarily occupied in the public world of paid employment and women located primarily in the home. She does not attempt to explain how this arrangement came about in the first place, but focuses on how it continues to be reproduced generation after generation. She claims that there are real personality differences between women and men, and that these are created and recreated by men's absence from the home, particularly when their children are very young. In the tradition of psychodynamic theory, Chodorow argues that women and men grow up to be different kinds of people because of the nature of the early relationships they have with their parents. She argues that the desire and capacity to mother a child (irrespective of one's sex) comes from having had good experiences of being mothered oneself as a child, and that there is in principle no reason why men should not have this capacity and desire. Chodorow's argument is thus based on how it is that men *lose* these.

The ability to parent originates, she says, in the 'primary love relationship' that the carer has with the child. In this early relationship, the child and parent are so bound up with each other that they don't experience much of a boundary between themselves, and this experience of 'oneness' is functional because it enables the parent to fully anticipate the child's needs. If we ourselves have had this primary love relationship as babies, when we grow up we should be able to recreate it with our own children. We are able to regress to this early kind of relationship for the benefit of our own children. So why do men so often seem to lack this capacity and desire?

In our present social and family arrangements it is women who are the primary caretakers and the problems begin here. Chodorow argues that mothers, who must bring up children of both sexes, experience their sons differently from their daughters. As women, they experience their daughters as similar to themselves, and this encourages them to prolong the primary love relationship with them. All children must eventually develop a sense of themselves as individuals separate from their parents, but this is delayed in daughters because of their mothers' strong sense of continuity with them, so that daughters are still to some extent embedded in this primary love relation even as they are establishing their own sense of self. The result of this is that girls' sense of self is actually defined in terms of empathy and relationship with others. Thus girls grow up with a strong capacity for experiencing others' needs and feelings as their own, and as adults they desire and can readily regress to a primary love relation with their own children.

However, boys have a more difficult time. Mothers experience their sons in terms of *difference*, and thus instead of prolonging the primary love relation with them they tend to curtail it. The boy's masculinity is the focal point for the mother's experience of him as different from her, and his maleness seems to stand out even more because her husband is absent from the home much of the time. As the boy grows up he begins to separate from his mother and develop a sense of self, but this sense of self is infused with the feeling of being masculine and *different* from his mother. For the boy, his developing sense of himself as masculine is forever bound up with the experience of separation and individuation. Moreover, he is at a loss to work out what being masculine might look like, since his father, as a potential source of identification, is generally absent. He can only rely on the feeling that it is most definitely the opposite of what he is familiar with – the femininity of his mother. To become masculine the boy then feels he must reject everything he associates with this femininity – the intimacy and empathy of the primary love relationship. Moreover, this rejection is reinforced by the Oedipal conflict, as the young boy comes to distrust and fear his growing sexual attachment to his mother. The outcome of all these forces is that the boy makes a decided and irrevocable break with femininity and all it represents. Because of the particular way in which their sense of self and of their own masculinity has been forced to develop, men as adults understandably fear regression to a primary love relationship – it threatens to undermine their masculinity and their very sense of themselves as individuals. It is for this reason, says Chodorow, that so many men find it difficult to establish emotional intimacy with their partners and why they are reluctant (and perhaps unable) to mother their children.

As a result both of being propelled into early separation and of their rejection of the family and its relationships as a place of emotional investment, men turn to the public sphere to seek their identity and the public/private divide becomes to them the symbol of their struggle to keep femininity at bay. It thus becomes important to keep the public world masculine and to keep women (and therefore femininity) safely contained within the private sphere. In this way the whole cycle repeats itself, and Chodorow argues that the way to break the cycle is through joint parenting, so that boys and girls would not in future grow up with a heavily distorted sense of self:

> Anyone who has good primary relationships has the foundation for nurturance and love, and women would retain these even as men would gain them. Men would be able

to retain the autonomy which comes from differentiation without that differentiation being rigid and reactive, and women would have the opportunity to gain it.

(Chodorow, 1979: 218)

Chodorow's account certainly puts forward the view that women and men are very different kinds of people, but that these differences are the product of social structures and practices. It gives us a way of understanding the different positions of women and men in society which goes beyond the views that these differences are simply the product of power inequalities or of social expectations, by suggesting how masculinity and femininity might become written into our psychology. The strength of this is that it explains why women and men often feel themselves to be suited to different kinds of work. For example, Marshall and Wetherell (1989) interviewed both male and female law students, and found that many of the women had to resolve an apparent conflict between femininity and becoming a lawyer. Their personal qualities were sometimes seen as inconsistent with the typical masculine lawyer, although some of them anticipated that the law would benefit from a feminising influence, and I think that this is consistent with Chodorow's view.

### Radical feminism

While Chodorow sees the achievement of more equal roles between men and women in the family as the way forward, Shulamith Firestone, a radical feminist, advocates the demolition of the family as we know it. She takes women's biological reproductive function as her starting point, but her analysis is not a reductionistic one. Like Chodorow, she argues that there is an interaction between individual and social forces. Firestone (1971) says that women's function as childbearers and childrearers has determined their position in the family, and this led to the establishing of patriarchy. Patriarchy thus originated with the very earliest families. She points to the long history of the biological family, in which women and their children depend upon men for survival. Throughout most of human history, women have had little or no control over reproduction. Multiple pregnancies and the consequent nursing of babies and young children would have made them dependent upon men for protection and food. Human infants need a long period of adult care, and bearing and nursing children for long periods, says Firestone, resulted in mothers and children developing a psychological interdependency akin to the 'primary love relation' described by Chodorow. This created the opportunity for men to establish the patriarchal structures and practices that we see today. Women's psychological investment in pregnancy and children restricted their activities and left them dependent upon men. Men took advantage of this situation to free themselves of responsibilities and to build a public world for their own use and benefit:

> Nature produced the fundamental inequality – half the human race must bear and rear the children of all of them – which was later consolidated, institutionalized, in the interests of men. . . . Women were the slave class that maintained the species in order to free the other half for the business of the world.
>
> (Firestone, 1971: 232)

She goes on to say that this led to women and men each sacrificing half of their potential as human beings, giving rise to exaggerated masculine and feminine psychological types. In this idea her account draws upon the notion of androgyny popular at the time (see Chapter 6). Firestone's solution is a biological revolution. Women must be freed from their reproductive relation with men and from their own psychological investment in pregnancy and childcare. She recommends that we develop reproductive technologies that will enable us to destroy the biological link between mothers, fathers and children. She believes that this would give rise to a society where there would seem to people to be no good reason why it should especially be mothers who have to or want to look after children – all adults would do their share. Firestone's view is useful because it takes account of biological and psychological differences between the sexes in a non-reductionistic way, although it is not without its problems. For a critical analysis of these, see Walby (1990).

Firestone focuses upon reproduction and mothering as the key factors in patriarchy, but other radical feminists see domestic labour as the issue. Theorists such as Christine Delphy argue that inequalities in the domestic division of labour exist and are hard to change because men benefit from them in two ways: they derive their own domestic comfort from women's domestic duties while at the same time handicapping women who want to compete with men in the public sphere. According to Bryson,

> From this perspective, men's resistance to change and their refusal to help with domestic chores ... were only to be expected, and quarrels about who should do the washing were not individual disagreements but part of a wider power struggle.
>
> (Bryson, 1992: 198)

Delphy (1980) argues that marriage is a form of labour contract, where women 'agree' to perform unpaid domestic duties. Men thus become women's economic masters and exploit their labour. As a result of their domestic position (as a class), women cannot compete in the market for paid work and marriage comes to seem the best economic option for them.

## Summary

Women and men still do not enjoy equality, either in the workplace or in the family, and the New Man may be more of an illusion than a reality. Both psychological accounts and feminist theories can go some way to explaining this state of affairs. Socialisation theory shows how girls and boys can grow up with different attributes, skills and expectations which may propel them along different life paths. Such socialisation begins so early and is so endemic in our culture that its results can appear to be natural. However, this does not explain the difference in status and access to material resources (e.g. pay) between the sexes. Equity and exchange theories, which regard the domestic divison of labour as a rational solution to a common problem, are adequate for only relatively few contemporary households. Feminist theories, on the other hand, tend to explain inequalities in terms of social structures (like capitalism and patriarchy). Although they differ in the extent to which they see class relations or gender relations as at the root of these, they offer tenable explanations of gender inequalities and show how women's and men's positions in paid work and the family are related. However, neither they nor socialisation theory adequately explains women's and men's different psychological investments in family and work. Few theories have attempted to address this problem, but Chodorow and, to a lesser extent, Firestone have tried to do this and offer ways of understanding how these 'investments' are bound up with inequalities.

## Further reading

Firth-Cozens, J. and West. M. (eds) (1990) *Women at Work: Psychological and Organizational Perspectives,* Buckingham: Open University Press. A wide range of articles on general issues, problems and women's experiences in specific occupations.

Hood, J. (ed.) (1993) *Men, Work and Family,* Newbury Park, Calif.: Sage. A good collection of chapters examining men's contribution to domestic labour and its relation to paid work.

Chapter 5

# Representations and language

IMAGES OF WOMEN AND MEN, whether written, spoken or visual, suffuse our everyday lives. Sometimes these very obviously carry stereotypical messages about the sexes, and so it is not surprising that, for example, pornography or television advertising have attracted criticism for the way they represent (and misrepresent) gender roles and relations. However, it may be argued that gender messages are also transmitted in much less obvious ways, and that questionable assumptions about women and men, and relations between them, are present in sources we might think of as quite harmless and indeed may even be embedded in the very language we speak.

Identifying the existence of such images does not in itself demonstrate that they are instrumental in bringing about gender differences and inequalities, and there is some debate over the extent to which such messages are really taken in by people. Male and female models in the child's environment have been thought to be a prime source of sex-role information (Kohlberg, 1966; Mischel, 1966) and the mass media are a rich source of such potential models. Other writers argue that the media are used and read in different ways by different individuals and that we cannot make assumptions about their effects. In this respect the situation is similar to the debate over the harmfulness of television violence. This is a debate which in the end cannot adequately be resolved through empirical (and in particular positivistic) research. There is no ethical or practical way of isolating the possible effects of representations in order to observe them.

However, in trying to understand how such images might be influential, it seems fair to say that we cannot take as our model the 'hypodermic syringe'; people do not simply and straightforwardly act upon messages to which they have been exposed. Those who argue that we should take gender representations seriously do not always fully theorise how this influence operates at a psychological level. Nevertheless, they have identified several issues which deserve consideration and which suggest that we cannot assume representations to be disconnected from the real world and its inequalities.

## Gender roles and status

### Children's reading material

Several studies in the 1970s and 1980s used an objective way of comparing images of women and men, by counting the number of pictures (in a book) or characters (in a story). They found that in children's books there are generally fewer representations of females than males and in stories there are more male characters, even where the characters are animals. Whereas some stories have no female characters, the reverse is rarely true. It is argued that this at least creates the impression that, both in real and fictional worlds, women are not central to the action.

A more **qualitative** approach has been to perform content analyses to reveal the messages embedded in these representations. This is necessarily a less objective approach, but has resulted in a wealth of rich information not available through more objective means. Such studies (e.g. Lobban, 1975) have tended to find that women and men are represented in quite different ways. Analyses of children's stories have found that female characters appear as passive compared to active male characters, engage in a narrower range of activities and that these tend to be associated with a domestic role. In stories, boys often have adventures but girls need to be helped or rescued.

Although early studies raised awareness about the stereotyping in children's books and led to some redressing of the balance, more recent studies suggest that it is still a problem and is not restricted to story books. Swann (1992) reports several studies which found, as in Lobban's earlier classic study, that school reading schemes and text books also under-represented girls and women and showed them in predominantly domestic or caring roles. As well as potentially transmitting the messages that different kinds of behaviour are appropriate for each sex and that the activities of boys and men are more worthy of attention, stereotypical images in text books may reinforce gendered subject choices at school (see Chapter 3). For example, Swann cites Hardy (1989) who analysed the *Look* primary science scheme. Although the representations of girls and boys were quite well balanced, adults tended to be male and female adults were often portrayed as incompetent or silly, and Hardy concludes that such images may reinforce girls' sense of alienation from science.

### Television

In major reviews of the literature available at the time, both Courtney and Whipple (1983) and Gunter (1986) found similar evidence of stereotyping in advertising and television programmes. The situation appears to be similar to that found in children's books. Women were greatly outnumbered by men and they were shown in a more limited range of (often domestic) roles. In advertisements, men were often shown as experts or advising women, and men were much more frequently used for voiceovers to recommend products. The situation is similar, although not quite as bad, in radio advertisements (Furnham and Schofield, 1986). Women in children's television programmes were portrayed as primarily concerned with their homes and families, preoccupied with their appearance, and, if employed outside the home, were likely to be seen in low status occupational roles. It is suggested that, if such representations influence children at all, the effect is to reinforce the status quo. In addition, actions instigated by males were shown as more successful or more likely to be rewarded than those instigated by females, which has important implications if children identify with characters of their own sex.

In adult drama, there were many fewer female central characters. This was not true for soap operas, but here women were mostly shown in highly stereotypical ways. Television programmes typically represented the world as even more rigidly gendered than it actually is, and did not reflect the changes in occupational roles and family type and organisation that have occurred since the

Second World War. Marriage and parenthood were depicted as of prime significance in a woman's life and men were much more likely to be depicted in work-related interactions. Men were typically depicted as having control over the situations they found themselves in, whereas women were shown having things 'happen to' them.

However, Gunter also very usefully reviewed research which has attempted to study how audiences respond to such messages, and argues that people do not passively absorb these. Perceptions of television characters were influenced by people's own perceptions of themselves, and there was a high level of awareness that the stereotypical roles and characteristics portrayed on television are not a true reflection of real life. Interestingly, audiences perceived male characters as so unrealistically masculine as to be beyond the achievement of ordinary people, whereas female characters were seen as more realistically human. However, Courtney and Whipple (1983) are inclined to find persuasive the experimental evidence concerning the extent of social learning from television, and argue that exposure to counter-stereotypical images in advertising could help to change children's expectations of themselves.

Although we may wish to draw back from assuming that audiences simply soak up gender messages, or straightforwardly model themselves on television characters, nevertheless there may be other ways in which television fiction is influential. In a study by Buckingham (1993), he suggests that children's talk about the programmes they watch is perhaps more important than the programmes themselves. In his research he found that, when discussing television programmes aimed at them, young boys' interactions with each other were a powerful means of constructing their own masculinity and displaying it to other boys. In the same volume, Walkerdine and Melody (1993) argue from a psychoanalytic perspective, suggesting that our fantasies, hopes and anxieties, are powerfully engaged with in popular fiction and that these stories can take the role of a 'relay point' through which we attempt to grasp and resolve the tensions and conflicts thrown up by our position as subjects in class and gender structures. In this view, watching television fiction may be a helpful way of imaginatively playing out our desires and fears, but at the same time may encourage us to invest ourselves in gendered identities which are portrayed as offering the route to true happiness.

In a similar vein, but taking a more social-psychological approach, Durkin (1985) puts forward the script as a model for understanding the relation between television and its audience. A script can be thought of as a socially recognisable way of organising an interaction or event (such as a meeting, a family meal or a romantic encounter). Without specifying exactly what each person is expected to say, there is a general pattern to an event which is recognisable, and we develop a personal repertoire of such scripts for use in everyday interaction. With respect to television fiction, this recognition of a script by viewers is vital if they are to engage with the story. Durkin argues that traditional gender roles feature strongly in some of the most popular media scripts such as the love story or the family drama, and that our personal repertoire of scripts that we use in daily interaction mesh with these to enable us to engage with the story. Although he does not fully articulate the process whereby gendered media scripts may influence viewers, Durkin offers an interesting alternative to the usual social learning model which gives full value to the active participation of the viewer.

Goffman (1976) analysed visual images of women and men used in advertising. He looked at a variety of still photographs in advertisements taken from North American newspapers and magazines, and identified a number of patterns with respect to how the sexes were represented. He found that these images were composed in such a way as to suggest status differences between the sexes. Except where this involved domestic tasks, men were shown in an executive role, showing women how to do things. Women were often situated physically below men in the photographs, suggesting an inferior position. In addition, he found that the posture of women in such photographs, particularly how the head was held, was unlike that of men. The head was typically slightly lowered and tilted to one side suggesting ingratiation or appeasement, and women were often shown in poses suggesting a childlike cuteness.

Goffman recognises the difficulty in postulating a relationship between such images and gender relations in real life, but argues that their very ordinariness is significant:

> Although the pictures shown here cannot be taken as representative of gender behaviour in real life ... one can probably make a significant negative statement about them, namely, that as pictures they are not perceived as peculiar and unnatural
>
> (Goffman, 1976: 25)

Thus, if we notice nothing odd or unusual in these images, this is likely to be because we (perhaps non-consciously) make the same assumptions about women and men as those that are being presented. In order to expose our own assumptions, Goffman recommends that we try imagining that the sex of the actors in an advertisement is reversed, and observe our own responses to the changed meanings this brings about.

Most of the research into sex-role stereotyping in the mass media was carried out in the 1970s and 1980s, and an important question is therefore whether media representations of women and men have changed substantially since then. Television advertising in particular has become more sophisticated, employing a wide variety of selling techniques, and the roles and characteristics of women and men now shown are often quite different from those a decade or so ago. Further research is needed in order to reveal whether these changes mark a move away from potentially damaging representations of both women and men.

### Women's magazines

Publications for women have been available since the seventeenth century, and women's magazines now constitute a hugely profitable industry. These purport to address women's interests, and magazines addressing men's interests do not exist in the same way. This is interesting in itself; Ballaster *et al.* argue that 'From their inception, women's magazines have posited female subjectivity as a problem, and themselves as the answer' (Ballaster *et al.*, 1991: 172), representing the reality of women's lives but also offering them certain ideals to live up to. Also, women's lives are seen as operating within the confines of home and personal relationships:

> Women's concern, according to most magazines, is with personal and emotional relationships, primarily with husbands or partners, but also with children, family and friends. The work of maintaining healthy personal relationships is women's work.
>
> (Ballaster *et al.*, 1991: 137)

Ferguson (1983) analysed the content of three women's magazines (*Woman, Woman's Own* and *Woman's Weekly*) over the period 1949 to 1980. In magazines from the first twenty years of this period she found a number of recurrent themes: 'getting and keeping your man', 'keeping the family happy', 'the working wife is a bad wife', 'self-help', 'overcoming misfortune and achieving perfection', and 'be more beautiful'. In the latter twenty years, social changes were reflected in the content of the magazines so that issues such as contraception and combining marriage with paid work were addressed. However, Ferguson found that the traditional ideas about femininity, values and women's roles remained much the same. The challenge was now seen as how to combine these with the new freedoms, giving rise to the concept of the modern superwoman who could manage to balance the demands of both home and career. Nevertheless, the message was still one which placed women's centre of gravity in the sphere of marriage and family:

> Orgasm thus makes a woman a better partner for her man, labour outside the home makes family or private life more exciting or more egalitarian, financial independence ensures that children can be supported despite the feckless nature of the opposite sex.
>
> (Ballaster *et al.*, 1991: 172)

## Gender relations

### *Heterosexuality in fiction*

As well as imparting messages about the relative status and roles of women and men, fiction for both adult women (such as stories and serials in women's magazines, and also Harlequin and Mills and Boon romances) and stories in teenage magazines present a particular image of the nature of relations between women and men. Again using a psychoanalytic framework, Walkerdine argues that the potential influence of media representations cannot be understood by the usual theories of socialisation and modelling. She argues that such representations are effective because they operate on women's *desire*:

> Cultural practices do not simply engage in a process of imposing normalization. They participate in the formation of desire, fuelling its flames, and thereby canalize it, directing it toward investment in certain objects and resolutions.
>
> (Walkerdine, 1987: 117)

Walkerdine analysed stories from two popular (at that time) comics for girls, *Bunty* and *Tracy*. She argues that, like classic fairy tales, these stories typically involve a heroine who must endure injustice and victimisation from others (perhaps a cruel stepmother or school bullies). The heroine's goodness, virtue and selflessness throughout this adversity are rewarded. Her difficulties are resolved and, by virtue of her passivity and compliance, she finally gains her rightful place in a longed-for 'happy family'. Walkerdine argues that such stories prepare girls for adolescent heterosexuality, where 'getting a man' offers potential escape from conflict and victimisation (perhaps at home or at work). Importantly, this is again achieved through the girl's attention to others' needs:

> Girls ... rise above their circumstances by servicing and being sensitive to others. The girl who services is like the beautiful girl whose reward for her good deeds is to be freed from her misery by a knight in shining armour. The semiotic chain slides into romance as the solution, with the

knight as saviour. Servicing helps to reproduce the autonomy of men and children. It is here that girls are produced as victim ready to be saved. Cruelty and victimization are the key features . . . that are salient in the production of women as passively sexual.

(Walkerdine, 1987: 111)

It is not surprising, therefore, that the predominant theme in teenage magazines is 'getting and keeping your man', where romance is the resolution to teenage girls' desire (McRobbie, 1982). As with comics for younger girls, the trials and tribulations (this time of love and romance) must be endured and the heroine must hope and have faith that 'Mr Right' is just around the corner. Modleski (1984) (cited in Ballaster *et al.*, 1991) identifies striking similarities in adult romantic fiction. Typically, the hero appears at first somewhat cruel and contemptuous, but is won over and mellowed by the passive virtue of the heroine.

However, McRobbie (1991) argues that we should be very careful about assuming how stories are read by people, and demonstrates that individuals take up meanings in such stories in very different ways. The researcher who identifies an 'ideological message' therefore cannot assume that this is the message perceived by the reader. Likewise, Moss (1993) argues that teen romance stories are read in quite different ways by girls, depending upon their other reading habits and familiarity with the genre. Nevertheless, Ballaster *et al.* (1991) make the point that in order to engage with a story at all, certain assumptions have to be held by the reader. In order to join in the celebration of other women's joys (e.g. at the birth of a longed-for child or in the result of a make-over) we have to accept, to some degree, the values and assumptions from which these spring: 'The magazine determines the range of possible meanings and assumptions implicit in its own text, what kind of life is seen as a struggle, as what is easy, or can be taken for granted' (Ballaster *et al.*, 1991: 131). Indeed, a number of traditional themes are so ubiquitous in stories and fairy tales that even non-traditional tales may be 'read' in traditionally gendered ways. For example, Davies and Harré (1990) found that when children were asked to read a non-traditional fairy tale (*The Paper Bag Princess*), they struggled to make sense of it in terms of the traditional gender patterns which they clearly assumed to be present.

Girls' and women's fiction has therefore been subjected to a great deal of analysis, prompted in part by a concern over its possibly damaging effects. Concern over literature for boys and men has been less obvious, and this is under-researched by comparison. It might be said that pornography, which I briefly consider below, is the exception but again the emphasis here has been very strongly upon theorising its possible damage to women.

### Masculinity, femininity and sexuality in visual representations

In analysing visual images, several writers have focused particularly upon the portrayal of women's and men's bodies, and have offered interpretations of these which have important implications for masculinity, femininity and sexuality. Berger (1972) argues that pictures of men's bodies convey quite a different message to those of women's bodies, such that men's bodies are for action and women's bodies are for looking at. The words we use to talk about attractive men and women also signify this. We say that a man is 'handsome', which literally means 'fit for the hand' or 'useful' but we describe a woman as 'beautiful' and beauty is 'in the *eye* of the beholder'. Typical pictures which represent the male body are found on the sports pages of daily newspapers. Here, the message is one of dynamism, of men in action. The bodies in these photographs display hard, straight lines and convey an impression of potential power. Berger argues that when we view these body images, we are not being invited to look at them in desire but to admire and celebrate the masculine ideals of power, agency and the mastery of mind over body. Such pictures of men, Berger argues, seem to portray a paradoxical disregard for the viewer. The men seem preoccupied with what they are doing, and the viewer appears to be an accidental onlooker. By contrast, pictures of women's bodies, he says, are essentially for looking at. Their bodies are displayed in such a way as to turn them into a visual spectacle, a sight. Furthermore, the attitude of the model in the photograph makes this relation with the viewer explicit. She looks out of the photograph at the viewer, knowing that she is being observed, and seems to ask 'do you like what you see?':

> One might simplify this by saying: *men act* and *women appear*. Men look at women. Women watch themselves being looked at. This determines not only most relations between men and women but also the relation of women to themselves. . . . Thus she turns herself into an object – and most particularly an object of vision: a sight.
>
> (Berger, 1972: 47, italics in original)

Berger therefore sees visual images as representative of relations between men and women in the real world. The feminist Rosalind Coward argues that advertisements and features in women's magazines encourage women to see their bodies as a kind of project. Each small body part is given attention by talking about what products may be used on it to improve its appearance or feel and women worry about the adequacy of their figures, their faces or their hair. Berger claims that women have thus inter-nalised the 'to-be-looked-at' model of themselves that is so widely on offer in representations, so that girls grow up learning to look at themselves, and to look at themselves through men's eyes. They are constantly self-monitoring:

> A woman must continually watch herself. She is almost continually accompanied by her own image of herself. Whilst she is walking across a room or whilst she is weeping at the death of her father, she can scarcely avoid envisaging herself walking or weeping. From earliest childhood she has been taught and persuaded to survey herself continually . . . because how she appears to others, and ultimately how she appears to men, is of crucial importance for what is normally thought of as the success of her life.
>
> (Berger, 1972: 46)

From this perspective, women's concern with their clothes, make-up and so on are not trivial issues but are signposts to the general nature of gender relations and sexuality. Taking a broadly psycho-analytic approach, Easthope (1986) suggests how this production of women as visual objects might be implicated in gender relations. He sees men's 'looking' at pictures of women as essentially motivated by a deep-seated fear first of femininity, which is in turn prompted by their anxiety to be properly masculine, to be real men, and second a fear of women, who men regard as having a dangerous sexual power capable of making them lose control of themselves. Easthope sees masculinity as a fragile construction which is defined primarily in terms of its contrast to femininity, rather as Chodorow does (see Chapter 4). In men's anxiety to be certain of their own masculinity, they must devise ways of ensuring first that masculinity and femininity are readily distinguishable from each other and cannot be confused. Their task is then to rid themselves of any sign of femininity and to make sure that the feminine and womanliness are kept safely at bay.

Men's efforts to avoid any confusion between masculinity and femininity, which is a homophobic fear, give rise to the polarisation of body characteristics that we associate with women and men. If men have body hair, women's must be removed. If men's bodies are hard and angular, the ideal feminine form must be soft and curved. As pointed out in Chapter 1, it is possible to see this polarisation operating in a variety of everyday contexts, from his n' hers styles of personal possessions and accessories such as wrist-watches, slippers and so on (which are also made to embody the associated masculine and feminine characteristics such as angularity or softness) to gender-specific spellings of the same name. In these ways, men can feel that their own bodies are safe from contamination by femininity.

Having achieved this separation of masculinity and femininity, femininity becomes located in women, who then become the bearers of and come to signify all that is threatening to masculine identity. Women and their femininity must be constantly kept under control, constantly supervised. Easthope argues that pictures of women serve this function for men. Icons such as Marilyn Monroe, he suggests, are important because they are beautiful women who represent the epitome of femininity. They signify the ideal of the perfect woman, and in this sense stand in for all women. If such a woman and her femininity can be controlled and held in surveillance, then by implication all womanhood and femininity can be kept safely at bay. Thus, men's desire to look at pictures of women is a desire to literally 'keep an eye on' women, to keep them and their femininity under surveillance. In this way they can at least create the feeling that they retain some power and control.

Root (1984) further argues that the construction of women's sexuality takes place partly through this 'looking', in men's use of pornography. She says that the excitement of these pictures lies partly in the thrill of the 'peephole' show, the thrill of observing someone who is unable to return your gaze. Pornographic pictures serve a double purpose for men, since the women portrayed in them are safely pinned down on the printed page but at the same time the model's invitational expression offers a man the illusion that she (and her sexuality) exists only for him. She argues that it is in this sense that pornography turns women into sexual objects for men. It is not simply that a woman in this context loses her personhood and becomes a thing, but that her very existence becomes defined in terms of men's desire. The picture and the model's invitational expression serve to feed the fantasy that women are principally beings who serve male desire. This is consistent with the view put forward by Brittan and Maynard (1984) in Chapter 2.

Furthermore, Root argues that pornography should not be viewed as abnormal in the sense of being dislocated from what is thought of as normal, everyday life. In the same way that some feminists view rape as an extreme form of usual relations between women and men, Root suggests that pornography is in essence very similar to the images which may be seen on countless advertising hoardings and found in abundance in women's magazines. The same message of female passivity and availability stares out from the fashion pages of *Cosmopolitan* and *Bella*. The postures and facial expressions used by fashion models are often indistinguishable from those found in pornographic magazines.

Many feminists such as Andrea Dworkin and Catherine Mackinnon have argued forcefully for the control and censorship of pornography. Dworkin (1981) claims that through pornography's themes of violence and domination men become desensitised to these and can let themselves believe that women enjoy pain and humiliation. MacKinnon (1989) goes further, denying the usual feminist claim that rape is not about sex but about power. She argues that in our patriarchal society the two cannot be separated; both women and men acquire their gender identity and sexuality within a social context of domination and submission, so that these issues become bound up with our sexuality. She goes as far as suggesting that social practices in which men oppress women are sexually gratifying for men. In this view, pornography mirrors the nature of men's sexuality. Other writers, such as Feminists Against Censorship, argue instead that 'we should criticise images of women in soap operas, women's magazines and fashion photographs, because more people see them and because they are thought of as part of "real life" whilst everyone knows that pornography is a fantasy world.' (from 'Pornography: There's no simple answer', a leaflet published by Feminists Against Censorship).

## Language and discourse

It is often assumed that language is simply a tool which enables us to express our thoughts and ideas. In this view of language as a vehicle for thought, language itself is a neutral, value-free system. However, there are alternative conceptions of the relationship between language and thought, both older and more recent, which claim that language is fundamental to the way we think. The Sapir–Whorf hypothesis, formulated in the 1920s and 1930s, states that language can determine thought and behaviour and that different kinds of language can shape different views of the world. Sapir and Whorf were anthropological linguists and were not primarily concerned with gender issues, but with cross-cultural differences in language and forms of life. Although the strong form of this hypothesis has attracted much criticism, a more moderate form (that language can influence thought and behaviour) is more widely accepted. More recent theoretical formulations deriving from postmodernism, such as **social constructionism** and discourse theory (see below), see language and all symbolic forms as providing the very concepts with which we think. Here, thought and language are seen as inseparable, and the forms of representation we use in daily life, including our spoken and written language, embody and reproduce power relations (including gender). In all these views, language is by no means a trivial matter. Academic debates about what we should say and to whom are thus highly relevant to our deliberations concerning changing attitudes and attacking inequalities. Language and its everyday use is here seen as having a key role in the production and reproduction of society and its inequalities, and language and social practices are seen as inextricably bound up with each other. This production and reproduction of gender and its inequalities is seen as operating both in the ways that language is used in interpersonal interactions and in the representations of women and men that are embedded in the very form and content of our native language.

### Gender in interpersonal interactions

The forms of address that we use when we speak to someone vary according to the relation between us. Those with whom we are on relatively intimate terms, such as members of our family and our friends, call us by our first names but where the relationship is distant or involves a status difference we are more inclined to use someone's title, such as Dr or Miss. Children, by virtue of their lower status with respect to adults, are normally addressed by their first names but may be required to address adults (other than their family) using their titles. In organisations, it is permissible for managers to call their staff by their first names, but the reverse would be considered unacceptably familiar and even insubordinate. Cameron (1992) notes that these markers of subordination and familiarity are present also in interactions between the sexes. She argues that women tend to be called by their first names more so than men and are much more likely to be addressed with terms of endearment such as 'love' or 'dear'. A woman may use such terms to a man if she is older than him or intimate with him, but it appears more acceptable for a man to use such terms to any woman unless she is in some way in direct authority over him. Cameron argues that the use of such terms is a way of claiming familiarity and superiority. In answer to the argument that men are simply being friendly, she says:

> If a male customer my age is addressed as *sir* while I am *love*, that surely says something about the relative respect in which we are held.
>
> But, secondly, what do endearment terms mean? As I have suggested already, they connote intimacy. When used by strangers, therefore, they are inherently disrespectful. They are a unilateral declaration by the man that he need not trouble about the formalities expected between non-intimates.
>
> (Cameron, 1992: 106, italics in original)

She goes on to suggest that this is part of the phenomenon of invasion of personal space which men achieve through staring at women, standing too close to them or touching them and that women in this respect are treated in the same way as children, whose personal space is routinely violated by adults. She draws an interesting parallel here between men's form of address to women and the racist practice of stripping black people of their adulthood and dignity by addressing them as 'boy' or 'girl'. She also points out that 'street remarks' aimed at women, which often appear ambiguously hostile and flattering at the same time, serve both to control public space, into which women thus become seen as intruders, and to remind women that they are being watched by men and are subject to their scrutiny. Swann argues that even though comments on someone's appearance are normally intended to be pleasant, 'they also serve as a reminder that a woman's appearance is available to be commented upon and that the person giving the compliment is in a position to pass judgement' (Swann, 1992: 31–32).

There are many more words available to insult women than men, especially sexual terms, and this is consistent with the sexual double-standard. Anderson (1988) reports a study which identified two hundred and twenty words for a sexually promiscuous woman (such as 'slag' and 'tart'), but only twenty for men and these (such as 'stud') are more likely to carry a positive connotation. Terms such as 'slag', like words which denote women as sexual prey (like 'tail' and 'crumpet'), have no male equivalents and words used to insult men are more likely to infer homosexuality or effeminacy. However, it must not be assumed that men are the only ones to use such terms when referring to women. Studies have revealed that such terms are widely used by adolescent girls to police their own sexual identities, showing that a girl's reputation is still a powerful force for social acceptance or rejection.

### Gender representations in language

In daily life as well as in newspapers and TV news reports, the language used to talk about women and men draws on different implicit representations of the sexes. As discussed above, the forms of address that we take for granted in our language embody subtle gender messages inviting us to view women and men differently; a man is normally referred to as Mr regardless of his marital status, whereas a women is called Miss or Mrs depending on hers. Implicit in these forms of address, therefore, is the assumption that when we hear about a woman and her activities her marital status is relevant to how we view these, and that this is not so for a man. This difference in emphasis is even more obvious in the typical manner that women and men are described in newspaper articles. Men are referred to by age and job, for example 'Mr Smith, 34, a computer analyst ...', whereas women are referred to by age and marital or family status, for example '19-year-old unmarried mother, Miss Jones ...' Assumptions about the roles of women and men can be subtly communicated through language. If we read a news article about 'managers and their wives', this assumes that managers are men and our mental image of the people represented is unlikely to include female managers. Similarly, reports which purport to describe the range of people involved in some event or disaster frequently make similar assumptions, for example 'passengers on the train included commuters, women and children'. Cameron (1995) cites the example of the former US president George Bush who, in defending the invasion of Panama, said 'we cannot tolerate attacks on the wife of an American citizen'. Cameron says: 'The problem here is that Bush simply did not think about women in connection with the category "American citizens" ' (p. 136).

Dale Spender was one of the first feminists to explore the sexist assumptions contained in our use of language, and is influenced by a very determinist reading of the Sapir–Whorf hypothesis. In her 1980 book *Man Made Language*, she argues that a variety of linguistic practices systematically make women and their experience invisible. Spender's main argument is that the development of language has been dominated by men and their concerns, and that culture and social practices have followed the assumptions laid down by language. The result is that in a variety of ways language simply does not allow for women's experience to be talked about, and often seems to assume that male experience is standard (and that female experience is abnormal or defective). There are lexical gaps where there exist no female equivalent of words which refer to men and their lives, particularly in the area of sexuality. For example, there are no female equivalents of 'virility' or 'emasculate'. Swann (1992) reports a survey of North American English which found that few words referred to women's experience of sex, and that many words for sexual intercourse implicitly assumed a male actor.

Where male and female versions of a word do exist, they often carry very different meanings (for example bachelor and spinster, master and mistress), and it is often the case that exclusively female words have a pejorative meaning. Many such words have acquired a derogatory meaning over time, and it is argued that these words come to take on such meanings because of their association with women. For example, 'hussy' used to mean the mistress of a house, or 'housewife'. This tends to happen to words which refer to any disadvantaged and relatively powerless groups, such as the disabled or mentally retarded (words like 'cretin' and 'moron' originally referred to specific ranges of measured intelligence).

Spender attacks the use of 'generic' words, such as 'man' to refer to all people and 'he' to refer to individual persons of either sex. Those who claim that this is unimportant often argue that everyone knows that these terms are meant to include women as well as men. However, this argument looks weak when we recognise the inappropriateness of possible sentences like 'Man is a mammal because he suckles his young.' Anderson (1988) reports numerous experimental studies which suggest that such 'generic' terms conjure up predominantly male images in the minds of their readers, and that therefore they are in practice far from neutral. Many writers recommend that we adopt instead gender-free terms such as 'human beings' or 'humankind', and use the plural pronoun 'they' instead of 'he' and 'she' for example 'When a person buys a lottery ticket, they are likely to overestimate their chance of winning.' In her utopian novel *Woman on the Edge of Time*, Marge Piercy invented the word 'per', to replace 'he' and 'she' to refer to a person of either sex.

Like the radical feminist Mary Daly, Spender argues that the only way for women to escape the confines of 'man-made language' is to develop their own language. This might include making up new, consciousness-raising words such as 'phallocracy' and 'her-story' or redefining pejorative terms as positive and desirable, much as the connotations of the word 'black' has changed by the use of phrases such as 'black is beautiful' and 'black power'. However, Spender has been criticised for her ambiguous position on social change (Cameron, 1992) since her heavily deterministic theory would seem to automatically exclude the possibility of women escaping the confines of 'man made language'. Daly, too, has been criticised on the grounds that she advocates a separatist withdrawal of women into a culture of their own, and one to which only educated middle class women could realistically have access.

Concern over the use of terms like 'man' and 'he', and also terms such as 'chairman' and 'manpower', has generated much argument over the issue of 'political correctness'. Those who have made extensive claims about the sexism (and racism) endemic in our language have triggered a backlash from others who argue that such claims are trivial or ridiculous, and that the words we use to refer to people in the end bear very little relationship to their position in society. However, Cameron (1995) argues that if such issues were indeed trivial they would hardly evoke the heated responses that they have. Some feminists have suggested that renaming things enables a redefinition of them that in turn brings about the possibility of thinking about things differently. For example, Bryson (1992) says that relatively new terms such as 'sexism' and 'sexual harassment' serve to redefine reality from a feminist perspective. Without such terms it would be more difficult for women (and indeed men) to identify and recognise certain experiences as oppressive. Throughout this book, I have used the phrase 'women and men' because reversing the usual order of presentation makes the phrase highly visible and therefore at least invites the reader to consider the assumptions hidden within our usual ways of speaking and writing.

### Social constructionism and discourse

The view that language has a directly formative influence on our thoughts and everyday assumptions about the world is central to social constructionism (see Burr, 1995), which is currently providing a postmodernist challenge to traditional psychology and social psychology. Social constructionism argues that our understanding of the world and each other is socially constructed through our interactions with each other, especially in our use of language, and that our thinking rests on the use of concepts and assumptions which are embedded in language. As with the strong form of the Sapir–Whorf hypothesis, the concepts we can use and what we can say we know are limited by the language (and therefore culture) we are born into. Social constructionism is by no means a unitary body of theory, but there are at least two strands of thought associated with it that are of interest in relation to gender.

The first is a concern with grammar, with the way that the structure of a language contains within it invitations to particular ways of thinking. This is essentially rather similar to what interested Sapir and Whorf. For example, in English our grammar always specifies, through tense, the point in time (past, present or future) at which the described events are presented as taking place. This means that our representations of events to ourselves and each other cannot be divested of the element of time, and time is thus such a background assumption for us that we cannot envisage a meaningful conversation where the order of events in time is not specified. Nevertheless, languages exist (for example that of the native American Hopi Indians) where the grammar is used to represent time only at the speaker's discretion but always distinguishes between events that the speaker personally witnessed and those that were reported to them by others.

Following through this line of reasoning, the very pronouns we use to refer to speakers ('I', 'you', etc.) create the space for us to think of ourselves as self-contained individuals, with different experiences and personalities. It is argued (e.g. Kitzinger, 1992) that this is not a universal way of thinking but one particularly prevalent in western industrialised societies. Words such as 'I' and 'you', and of course 'he' and 'she' open up what are referred to as 'subject positions' for speakers to fit into, offering them a perspective on the world and a way of thinking which arrives with the use of the language. The French psychoanalyst Jacques Lacan has drawn upon this view of language and has developed a complicated theory of how women and men become produced as gendered subjects through their acquisition of language as young children (for a clear overview of this theory see Cameron, 1992 or Frosh, 1987).

The second strand focuses on the identification of discourses (Foucault, 1972), which may be seen as coherent ways of representing the world (and people) through language and other symbolic means. Different discourses construct the world in different ways, and offer competing pictures of what people (and thus women and men) are like. They therefore offer different versions of knowledge. The hallmark of the social constructionist view here is that it posits an intimate relationship between knowledge and power, such that relatively powerful groups in society are able to give certain discourses the stamp of truth. For example, our usual understanding of health and illness is based on a biomedical model (which can be thought of as a discourse) and the medical profession remains powerful through its ability to systematically marginalise and discredit alternative conceptions (e.g. witchcraft, spiritual healing, etc.)

With regard to gender, it is argued that patriarchy rests on the widespread acceptance of certain discourses (discourses which construct femininity, masculinity and sexuality in particular ways) as truth and upon the ability of powerful men in society throughout history (e.g. in the church, the law and in government) to regulate what counts as the truth regarding the abilities and dispositions of the sexes, especially through their control of public discourse (e.g. scientific publications). It is important here to recognise that such discourses are not simply ways of talking, disconnected from what people actually do, but are bound up with social practices. For example, prevailing discourses of sexuality enable men who rape to be sympathetically seen as just 'doing what comes naturally' and for their victims to be thought of as 'acting provocatively'.

As with the other views of language outlined above, this view sees language as important to the question of social change. If our very identities and the relations between women and men are constructed through the language we use, then we can become different people and forge different relations by challenging dominant discourses and opening up linguistic spaces where marginalised (e.g. female, black, gay) ways of seeing the world can emerge.

## Summary

In this chapter I have considered various ways that our representations of the world are gendered. Throughout the mass media, in television, books, magazines and popular fiction, and also in our use of language there are undeniably differences in the ways we depict and refer to women and men. Numerous research studies have documented the nature and prevalence of stereotypical images in all of these areas, so that there seems no doubt that our major cultural forms embody assumptions about the sexes that many would wish to challenge. Nevertheless, the questions of how influential such representations are in how we behave toward each other and how we may understand the processes through which this influence takes place are not so easily answered. While social learning theory has been popular as a way of understanding the influence of media images, its usefulness is perhaps limited. We need to understand how people engage with media messages in the way that they do (and also why they don't) and some writers have drawn on psychoanalytic theory to do this. The question of influence takes a rather different turn when we consider language, with writers from a variety of backgrounds arguing that language (and the representations contained within it) heavily influences the way we think and perhaps even constitutes it. At the very least, the debate seems to have moved away from the older but unfruitful issue of whether people should be seen as either 'sponges' soaking up the messages embedded in representations and language or as 'users' impervious to them.

## Further reading

Cameron, D. (1992) *Feminism and Linguistic Theory* (second edition), Basingstoke: Macmillan. A comprehensive and thorough analysis of gendered language.

Durkin, K. (1985) *Television, Sex Roles and Children: A Developmental Social Psychological Account*, Milton Keynes: Open University Press. A classic book in the field, balancing psychological and sociological theory and research.

Dworkin, A. (1981) *Pornography: Men Possessing Women*, London: The Women's Press. Dworkin puts forward her radical feminist case against pornography.

Weedon, C. (1987) *Feminist Practice and Poststructuralist Theory*, Oxford: Blackwell. An accessible account of the construction of gender through language and discourse.

Chapter 6

# Gender and psychological research

## How has gender been researched by psychologists?

### Sex differences

Psychology's approach to the study of gender has, not surprisingly, been to regard gender as an intra-psychic phenomenon. That is, gender, like many other phenomena of human experience, has been thought of as part of a person's psychological make-up, like other aspects of their personality such as extraversion or self-esteem. Of course our experience of gender is a profoundly psychological one, but the important social and political aspects of gender have largely been ignored by psychologists and much of the research in this field therefore reflects this bias. This strong tendency to see gender as (no more than) an interesting personality trait has resulted in a great deal of research which documents a range of differences between women and men but has little that is useful to say about how these findings may be interpreted.

There has been a strong focus upon sex differences research in psychology (see Chapter 2), particularly in the 1960s and 1970s. This interest was partly driven by the growing popularity of psychometrics in psychology, but there also appears to be an underlying assumption, first, that women and men are psychologically quite different from each other, and second that these differences are of importance for our understanding of human behaviour and experience. This manifests itself in a tendency to build sex comparisons into research designs almost automatically, and, as I pointed out in Chapter 2, to over-report findings of significant difference and to under-report findings of similarity, despite the fact that significant differences may be numerically small.

### Masculinity and femininity

Apart from sex differences research, a second popular area of concern for psychologists has been the measurement of masculinity and femininity. Numerous scales and inventories designed to measure these were devised in the first half of this century, and, as might be expected, their designers often did not critically examine the assumptions upon which such scales were built. Constantinople (1973) provided one of the first critical reviews of such tests and, in her critique of these assumptions, paved the way for the emergence of the concept of 'psychological androgyny' (Bem, 1974; see below).

Early measures made the assumption that masculinity and femininity comprised the two poles of a single dimension (masculinity–femininity). This meant, both in theory and in research practice, that being masculine necessarily meant being non-feminine and vice versa. Therefore a man's masculinity was conceptualised in terms of his *distance* from femininity, and it would be theoretically impossible, for example, for a woman to become more masculine without losing some of her femininity. The dimension is thus based on a system of opposites, so that any trait associated with one pole could not, by definition, be associated with the opposite pole. For example, if masculinity is associated with rationality then femininity must imply irrationality.

Constantinople criticised this masculinity–femininity concept on a number of grounds. The content of the scales indicated a very woolly definition operating behind them. Researchers either simply drew upon their own common sense notions of what masculinity and femininity were, and in this they were inevitably influenced by the normative practices of their own culture, or more usually they relied upon empirically derived criteria (as in the Terman and Miles Attitude–Interest Analysis Test and the masculinity–femininity (M–F) scales of both the Strong Vocational Interest Blank and the MMPI), so that their indices of masculinity–femininity were those that statistically discriminated between men and women. While the latter may appear more scientifically defensible, they were often psychologically meaningless since the face-validity of the resulting scale items was sometimes negligible (that is, they appeared to bear little relation to what most people would think of as masculinity or femininity). Furthermore, despite their reliance upon scientific method, such scales still did not escape the criticism that they are heavily culture-bound, and inevitably draw on culturally prescribed behaviours for women and men.

The bipolarity that Constantinople criticised has the further disadvantage of effectively mapping gender onto biological sex. When items are used which simply discriminate statistically between men and women, the dichotomy of male–female slips like a glove onto that of masculinity–femininity. It thus becomes impossible to conceptualise a difference between femaleness and femininity, maleness and masculinity. Furthermore, an explicit assumption underlying some of these scales is the idea that masculinity and femininity are related to sexual orientation and pathology. It was assumed, without support from research evidence, that men who showed sex-inappropriate levels of femininity were homosexual and (therefore) sexually deviant. Thus, for example, the M–F scale of the MMPI was drawn up partly by using items which were found to reliably identify homosexual males.

### Psychological androgyny

Constantinople rightly asks whether masculinity and femininity can be taken to exist as properties of a person's psychology, or whether they are best regarded as socially constructed and rather arbitrary ways that human beings organise information arising from their social experience. The latter is a view which is more likely to find favour among gender theorists today, but at the time that Constantinople was writing the more pressing concern was to rid the masculinity–femininity construct of some of its more damaging implications. Although she finds the bipolar M–F construct unsatisfactory, she points out that at the time no scales existed which did not take this as a basic assumption, and that therefore the tenability of an alternative conceptualisation could not be researched. This challenge was taken up by Sandra Bem (1974) with the development of the Bem Sex-Role Inventory (BSRI).

Bem took on board the kinds of criticisms that Constantinople raised and designed a measuring instrument intended to overcome the damaging conceptions associated with the bipolar M–F dimension. In addition to being concerned to conceptualise masculinity and femininity as discrete dimensions and to separate them from biological categories, she was keen to challenge the view that sex-inappropriate masculinity and femininity are related to sexual and psychological pathology. There has been a long history in psychology, associated with psychodynamic theory, that the psychologically healthy person is appropriately sex-typed. Thus the woman who is unfeminine, often by virtue of her lack of desire for motherhood, is regarded as sick, as is the man who is drawn to traditionally feminine interests (and he is also regarded as sexually inverted, i.e. homosexual and thus sick in a different way).

Bem argued that the relationship between psychological health and sex-typing might actually be the reverse of that usually assumed. She drew on an increasing body of evidence suggesting that people who display extreme sex-typing are less well-adjusted than others. In particular, the evidence suggested that extreme femininity is potentially crippling for women, since many traditionally feminine traits are incompatibe with maturity and mental health (Broverman *et al.*, 1970). Bem argued that masculinity and femininity constitute psychological strait-jackets, and that in limiting ourselves to the prescriptions of these narrow roles a properly full and flexible repertoire of responses to our social environment is closed to us. Women and men who live according to these prescriptions are thus only half-people. Bem thought of 'androgyny' (an ancient Greek word from 'andro' meaning 'male', and 'gyn' meaning 'female'), a balance of both masculine and feminine traits, as the natural state of both women and men, and that this becomes distorted through the systematic repression of the 'opposite-sex' half of our personalities during socialisation. If we were able to draw on both masculine and feminine traits and behaviours, we would all be more well-balanced people.

In devising the BSRI, Bem rejected the method of finding items which discriminate between the sexes. Instead she used a panel of judges, who looked at a wide range of trait terms (such as 'understanding', 'self reliant', 'compassionate' and 'analytical') and were asked to assess the desirability of each of these for a man and for a woman. The judges' ratings were used to select the final items for the scale, which comprised 20 'feminine' items, 20 'masculine' items and 20 further neutral items (such as 'happy' and 'theatrical') to mask the others. A seven-point Likert-type scale was attached to each item, and respondents thus rated themselves on each trait term from one (never or almost never true) to seven (always or almost always true). Respondents therefore gained scores for both masculinity and femininity. Scores could range from 20 to 140 for each of these, which in effect became orthogonal dimensions (i.e. statistically unrelated, like the E and N dimensions of the EPI). It was now possible to locate people in one of four categories, according to their combination of M and F scores:

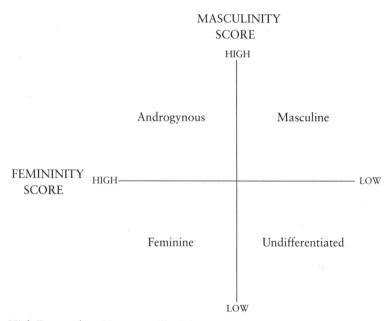

High F score, low M score  = Feminine
High M score, low F score  = Masculine
High F score, high M score  = Androgynous
Low F score, low M score   = Undifferentiated

*Criticisms of androgyny and the BSRI*

Bem saw the androgynous person as the most desirable type. The androgynous female would not be afraid to express her anger or trust her own judgement, and the androgynous male would not be afraid to show his emotions or to admit to weakness and vulnerability. But at the time that Bem was writing, one of the major concerns of feminists was the discrimination that women encountered in paid work, and in particular their restricted access to jobs which were thought of as requiring qualities particularly associated with men. Although the concept of androgyny is applicable to both sexes, its appeal for many lay in the possibilities it offered for demonstrating that women could have many of the same qualities as men and therefore do the same jobs. To the extent that sex discrimination was and is based upon widely held misconceptions about what women and men are like, this is an important point and should not be played down. Nevertheless, the concept of androgyny and the BSRI itself have received heavy criticism.

Although it may be an improvement on pre-existing ideas, it fails to ask why socialisation carries such a strong gender message and why the particular content of masculinity and femininity is as it is. It does not ask why society has been at such pains to repress certain characteristics in half the population and encourage them in the other half. In short, it fails to place individual psychology in the context of the material world and power relations. Hollway (1989) criticises Bem for implying that, if we all personally took the trouble to de-emphasise gender in our own lives and in bringing up our children, the differences between the sexes would eventually disappear and equality would follow. The ideas that people hold are thus seen as unconnected to the material reality that we inhabit. The great danger here is that the solution to the problem appears to be that of changing people's attitudes through education and information. However, it could be argued that there has in recent times been a substantial shift in the way people think about the sexes, and women in particular have undergone a transformation in what they think of as appropriate for themselves. Nevertheless, this has not led to the elimination of inequality. When the material world remains substantially the same despite changes in attitudes, there is a strong temptation for people to believe that gender inequalities must after all be biologically given.

Eisenstein (1984), a feminist, is critical of the way that existing traditional masculine qualities seem to have been unquestioningly accepted by Bem and written into the BSRI. She argues that 'the androgynous concept embodied an uncritical vision of maleness and masculinity: the qualities of aggression, competitiveness, leadership, and so on were taken to be good in themselves, and therefore important for all people to acquire.' (p. 63). In addition to the masculine traits mentioned above, traits such as gullible and yielding are questionable as desirable traits for women (or men, for that matter). The BSRI was constructed by asking a panel of judges to rate the desirability of traits for women and men. Although this was an improvement on previous methods of scale construction, it still necessarily draws heavily upon prevailing stereotypes and today we might well question the desirability of many of the traits included in the BSRI.

Moreover, Eisenstein argues that what we are seeing in instruments such as the BSRI is the psychologisation of power relations between the sexes. If we look at some of the BSRI items, it can be seen that they appear to refer to traits which are the property of individual psyches. For example 'dominant' and 'independent' appear as psychological characteristics which could, theoretically, be available to either sex. But these terms may more properly describe a pattern of social relations. To be dominant means to be in a positon of power over another person and to be independent means not being reliant upon others for resources. We do not, after all, explain the dominance hierarchies of apes in terms of their differing personalities. A person is in a position of dominance relative to another when the conventions of their society give one certain rights and powers over the other, or gives them greater access to recources. To refer to men's dominance and women's dependence as traits therefore misrepresents power relations as psychological characteristics and draws attention away from material inequalities.

Eisenstein doubts the advisability and possibility of combining masculinity and femininity in the same person on these grounds. She quotes feminists Janice Raymond and Jean Baker Miller, who make these points very succinctly: 'the language and imagery of androgyny is the language of dominance and servitude combined. One would not put master and slave language or imagery together to define a free person.' (Raymond, 1979: 161). The idea of androgyny, says Miller, 'remains a fanciful notion unless we ask seriously who really runs the world' (Miller, 1976: 79).

Bem's later writing showed a concern for some of the criticism that the concept of androgyny had attracted. Her goal was a genderless society, where the terms masculinity and femininity would cease to have any meaning and she moved away from androgyny, developing what she referred to as 'gender schema theory' (Bem, 1981). In this theory, she abandons masculinity, femininity and androgyny as personality traits that people possess in varying quantities, and instead conceptualises these as dimensions which we are accustomed to using in order to structure our world. Within the framework of this theory, the person who is highly sex-typed is one who tends to order and understand their world and themselves in terms of gender. Such people are therefore using a gender schema, and she reformulates her earlier recommendation that individuals become more androgynous, saying instead that society should become less gender schematic. Although this is an attempt to meet the criticisms levelled against androgyny, gender schema theory does not indicate how this change is to be brought about. However, in a much later book, Bem (1993) develops the idea that society sees the world through a number of gendered lenses (these being biological essentialism, androcentrism and gender polarisation) and puts forward a number of recommendations for how these may be challenged.

Despite the many difficulties with the concepts of androgyny and gender schema and the flaws in the BSRI, we should nevertheless value this attempt to replace the old M–F idea with less damaging concepts of masculinity and femininity, and the contribution this may have made to challenging commonplace gender stereotypes and work roles.

## How is the study of psychology 'gendered'?

### Androcentrism in psychological research

During the 1980s and 1990s a feminist critique of psychology and its methods has been gathering momentum. This has come primarily from women within the discipline of psychology. Although they do not necessarily share the same feminist theoretical allegiances, they are all concerned about how women and men are located within psychology, both as researchers and as the subjects of research, and there is now a substantial body of literature which discusses these issues (e.g. Hollway, 1989; Squire, 1989; Burman, 1990; Harding, 1991).

One of the major criticisms that has been made of psychology is that it is androcentric (centred on men and male experience). It is claimed that women have been systematically excluded from or misrepresented in research. Kohlberg's research on moral development (see Chapter 2) is often cited in this context, since Kohlberg developed his stage theory of moral reasoning using male subjects. Another example is research on lifespan development. When psychologists began to explore the idea that psychological development and change continued beyond childhood and adolescence, research which documented these changes focused upon the experience of men. For example Levinson (Levinson *et al.*, 1978), working in the USA, interviewed a number of men about their lives from childhood onwards. He identified common themes in their life histories, and from this he theorised that there are a number of developmental periods or transitions linked to chronological age ranges. Although later lifespan research was more sensitive to gender (and other) issues, much of the early research and theory was based on male experience (see Kimmel, 1980 or Rogers, 1986).

At its simplest level, the problem looks as though the obvious solution is to perform further research studies using women as subjects, in order to make sure that they are fully represented. However, the problem is more complicated than this because, as in the case of Kohlberg's and Levinson's research, the theoretical frameworks themselves were developed along masculine lines.

'Adding women in' to subsequent research may mean trying to fit women's experience into a masculine framework, which inevitably distorts it. It also has the effect of supporting the idea that male experience is normal or standard, so that women become readily seen as 'other', deviant and pathological. The attempts of well-intentioned feminist psychologists to redress the balance often left unquestioned the androcentric assumptions underlying some areas of research. For example, applied research on women managers left unchallenged the assumption that the (male) focus on assertiveness and problem-solving is legitimate (see Squire, 1989, for an overview and critique of feminist psychology). This problem is not of course confined to gender. Similar issues arise when psychologists use tests or theories developed using white, middle class males in the study of people from the working class or ethnic groups.

A second major criticism concerns the topics which are considered worthy of attention, both in research and in teaching. It is argued that the questions that psychology has focused upon have been those that have seemed relevant to men. It is argued that the agendas of psychology and social psychology, with their history of research and theory in areas such as achievement motivation, leadership, learning, thinking and problem-solving and intelligence measurement, have been set according to what seemed important questions to the (predominantly male) members of the discipline, as well as the governments and industrialists funding the research. Sherif (1987: 52) reminds us that:

> the military and other agencies of government have poured huge sums into research on problems that concerned them at the moment. ... The relationship between what was supported, what psychologists in those periods studied, and what problems were concerning government and the military is clear, though seldom discussed.

Ussher (1989, 1990) tells how her PhD work on menstruation and premenstrual syndrome was not regarded as real psychology by her male colleagues. She points out that the issues of menstruation, pregnancy and childbirth, although of obvious significance to women, were ignored in lifespan research. Kagan and Lewis (1990), writing about their experiences of teaching in a predominantly male psychology department, argue that topics such as interpersonal skills, which they wished to introduce into the curriculum, were perceived as softer and less rigorous than topics like cognition and were consequently marginalised. This marginalisation takes the form not simply of the expression of attitudes and opinions about the status of certain research topics, but operates very materially through editorial decisions to publish or not to publish such work in respected psychology journals (Spender, 1981), and through the decisions of funding bodies.

There has been a growing reaction against this state of affairs by feminist psychologists, who have been concerned to bring the study of women's experience back from the margins of psychology and to make it legitimate. The British Pychological Society (BPS), the professional body for psychologists in Britain, now has a Psychology of Women Section and very recently we have seen the formation of a Psychology of Lesbianism Section. In recent years there has been a steady rise in publications which explicitly aim to study women's experience in its own right and to avoid pathologising it by comparing it to a male standard. However, such feminist writing does not simply uncritically utilise existing psychological methodologies. Mainstream psychology has been referred to as 'malestream' to emphasise the general androcentrism of psychology. As we shall see, it is not only in its male-oriented subject matter and reliance upon male samples that psychology has been criticised. Some feminists argue that psychology is even more fundamentally gendered, and that its very foundations as a science, such as objectivity, systematic control of variables and value-freedom, are part of an ultimately male experience and vision of the world.

### Value-freedom and objectivity

Psychology has built its reputation on its success in modelling itself upon the natural sciences. The keystones of this vision of science are value-freedom and objectivity, the aims to ensure that our enquiries about the world are free from prior assumptions, vested interests and subjective interpretations. However, it may be argued not only that psychology is riddled with vested interests but also that the goals of objectivity and value-freedom themselves are unattainable fantasies.

Given the history of psychology and the fact that its funding has come from bodies with very vested interests, it seems plain that we should at least be cautious about assuming that the findings of research can be taken at face value. Sayers (1982) shows how in the past it was 'proven' that education would ruin women's reproductive capacities or that their smaller brains meant that they are intellectually inferior to men. We may smile at such ideas today, and can readily see the political game being played here, but there seems little reason to suppose that contemporary research, for example regarding brain asymmetry (see Star, 1991 for a critique of this) is fundamentally any different. The questions that have been asked of psychology and the answers that psychology has given us about women and men, it may be argued, have been heavily influenced by patriarchal concerns. This means that the very claim that psychology is apolitical (because it is assumed to be objective and value-free) is in itself a highly political one, since it obscures the role that psychology has played and continues to play in supporting existing power inequalities. Again, this point is relevant to a range of inequalities and is not limited to gender.

Even if we put this argument to one side, there is a more general point to be made concerning value-freedom and objectivity. Psychology (and science generally) creates the impression that there are certain problems that need to be addressed, and that there are 'facts' about the nature of the world which are lying around waiting for us to discover them through our scientific methods, which will help us to solve these problems. But there is really no such thing as a problem *per se*. A problem is always a problem *for* someone; and one person's problem is often another's solution. For example, we often hear that the breakdown of the family is a contemporary problem. Governments bemoan the rise in divorce rates and single parent families. These certainly are problems for the state, since they have implications in terms of provision of benefits and housing shortages, as well as having longer term implications for the role of the family in the provision of care for the elderly and so on. However, women's 'flight from the family', which is a large part of this state of affairs, is often to the women concerned a solution to their problems (oppressive marriages, abusive partners, etc.), which in their turn will not be experienced as problems by their menfolk. When such a state of affairs becomes defined as a problem, we must ask for *whom* this appears as a problem and whether some people have a greater power than others to decide just what constitutes a problem anyway.

Given that our enquiries are driven by the questions (problems) that seem to us, from our perspective (as governments, men, women or any other grouping) to exist, it follows that the kinds of answers that are available to us, the facts that we turn up, are going to be necessarily limited by this. We can only get answers to the questions we choose to ask. We can therefore begin to see that objectivity is a fiction. There never can be objective facts waiting for discovery. Facts are always the product of someone choosing to ask a particular question which in its turn rests on prior assumptions (for instance, that the family should be preserved, or that men and women must be different from one another).

Even if we could somehow magically guarantee that research findings are truly objective (which seems a logical impossibility, since no person is free to see the world from anything other than their own position in it) we would still have to face the issue of interpretation. The facts cannot ever speak for themselves, and must always be brought into being through the knowledge and assumptions of the researcher. As ordinary human beings, scientists are no different from anyone else when it comes to their participation in a shared culture and language (Hollway, 1989) and it is a fantasy to expect that we can divest ourselves of our culture's taken-for-granted assumptions by an act of will or by donning a white coat and practising scientific method. Findings that men are 'field independent' (which is positively valued) and

women 'field dependent' (seen as a handicap) might just as legitimately have been interpreted as showing that women are able to
take contextual features into consideration and men tend to take
things out of context. Research demonstrating the 'excessive talk-
ativeness' of women might just as easily have been interpreted as
demonstrating 'women's excellent verbal skills'. But the point is
that it was not (see Star, 1991).

The objectivity of science is further manifested through the
division operating between experimenter and subject and through
the adoption of the experiment as the preferred research design.
In research reports and scientific discourse generally, the
researcher and the persons being researched are represented in
very different ways. The researcher is the holder of knowledge,
the one who derives and tests theories and who is able to say
what the results mean. The subject, by contrast, merely responds
to the stimuli presented by the researcher and whose voice is
absent from the interpretation of her or his responses. In fact, the
supposed objectivity of the researcher is further manufactured
through the passive language of the journal report. Squire (1990a)
argues that this language obscures the activity of the researcher.
Psychologists may report that 'an experiment was performed',
(not that they performed an experiment), or that 'subjects were
exposed to stimulus material' (not that the researcher gave the
subjects the material). The presence, activities and expectations of
the researcher are thus removed from view.

As Howitt (1991: 52) points out, the use of the term 'subject'
in psychology is indicative of the power differential operating
between experimenter and subject:

> There are two significant implications of the use of the term
> 'subjects' that probably reveal more about psychology than
> a mere word should. First, people become merely objects to
> which something is done, thereby losing many of the features
> of their humanity – including having choice of action and
> being active rather than passive. Second, psychology is the
> realm of psychologists not of their subjects. So rather than
> psychology being what people who take part in research give

to other people conducting the research, it is separated from people and in the hands of those who *do* this sort of psychology to people. Very clearly this is a power relationship for the production of social knowledge.

(Italics in original)

The experimental method not only means that the experimenter and subject become split off from each other and caught up in an undemocratic relationship, but the subject additionally becomes stripped of context. The person is regarded as an isolable phenomenon that can be understood without reference to the social context which gives behaviour its meaning. This concern to rid oneself of a sense of connectedness with the world one inhabits and to construct the fantasy that one is separate and self-contained is seen by some feminists as a particularly masculine preoccupation. It can be seen that the decontextualisation and unequal power relationship described above are questionable, and that they may lead us to believe that psychology has not done justice to the perspective and agency of the people it has used in its research, irrespective of their gender, class or ethnicity. Nevertheless, it is arguable that where psychology has studied groups who are disadvantaged in society the effect is to make matters worse. Psychology has taken the experience of such people and stripped it of the social and material context which gives it its rationale, and has offered accounts of it which the people themselves have had no voice in producing and which have often served to bolster the inequalities they already suffer. The research into 'racial' differences in intelligence is a prime example. Likewise, psychologists have had the power to define women's experience in a way which locates as a personality trait or deficit (e.g. depressive personality or neurotic) that which may be more justly seen as a normal response to intolerable material circumstances.

## Rewriting the aims of psychological research

The arguments against the experiment as an appropriate research design for psychology are now well-documented, although they have had little impact in some quarters and the traditional paradigm still enjoys a privileged position. However, there has been a growing move among feminist psychologists (and others) to question the prevailing definition of science and to promote methods which are based upon very different assumptions about the aims and purposes of research.

The overarching concern is for a more democratic vision of research, where the aim is no longer for scientists to conduct studies *on* ordinary people and to discover facts about them (which may then be used against their interests) but to conduct research which is explicitly *for* people. The information-gathering purpose of research thus takes second place to a facilitative and liberatory one. With regard to studies of gender, feminists have attempted to redress the historical balance by conducting research which generates explanations that women themselves can own, understand and use to change their lives, not explanations useful to 'male' institutions such as medicine and the law. This model demands that the views and interpretations of the people being researched have as much (if not more) validity than those of the researcher. This concern is part of a more general one which has a fairly long history in social psychology. Those writing of the crisis in social psychology in the 1960s and 1970s (e.g. Brown, 1973; Armistead, 1974) were becoming increasingly concerned about power inequalities between researchers and their subjects and the silencing of the latter through the experimental method. There was therefore a growing enthusiasm for methods of enquiry which did allow the voice of the subject a place, giving validity to the person's experience and their account of it. There has therefore been a rise in the respectability and use of the qualitative (as opposed to quantitative) research methods in psychology, methods which have been widely used in other social sciences, such as sociology and anthropology, and where they are not seen as lacking in scientific rigour. Nevertheless, there is still undoubtedly in psychology a widespread perception that quantitative (or 'hard') data is somehow superior to qualitiative (often referred to as 'soft') data.

## *Interviewing and discourse analysis*

Depth interviewing has therefore become a popular method with researchers (including feminist researchers) who share this concern about documenting and legitimating people's accounts of their experience. However, although interviewing may appear to redress the balance, it is argued that textbook advice on how to conduct rigorous and valid interviews is based upon the same notion of dispassionate objectivity that infuses the experimental method. Oakley (1981b) draws on her own experience of interviewing women about their experiences of childbirth, and concludes that the process of conducting an interview is in practice very different from the recommended model.

Interviewers are supposed to operate only as recorders of information, and to minimise their own impact upon the respondents in order not to bias their responses. They are advised not to become too friendly with their interviewees or to talk about themselves. Oakley sees these recommendations as originating in the same masculine preoccupation with objectivity and detachment that underpins experimental method, and argues that successful interviewing cannot realistically achieve these ends and indeed should not try to do so. It is a fantasy that the interviewer can be thought of as an impersonal stimulus which evokes an uncontaminated or pure response from the interviewee. In reality, interviewer and interviewee are two elements in a whole system (the interview) in which the contributions and influences of each cannot be disaggregated. The point being made is that this does not render the interview biased and therefore invalid, and that all scientific inquiry involving people (including but not exclusively psychology) is necessarily embedded in a web of social relations from which it simply cannot be extricated. Laboratory experiments are no exception to this, and should be seen not as revealing examples of pure and unbiased behaviour, but as social enactments of a peculiar and particular kind involving their own sets of interpersonal relations, expectations and rules and producing responses which are very much the outcome of a rather unusual form of social interaction.

This view leads to the recommendation that as researchers we accept, work with and use this interconnectedness between researcher and researched. Breaking the rules of interviewing (for example allowing the researcher to offer their own experience or to answer personal questions) is thus seen as producing a more rather than less valid interview, and one where the role of the researcher is made explicit. For example, Tempest (1990), herself an adopted daughter, argues that if she were to legitimately and validly research the relationship between other adopted daughters and their mothers it would not be possible or desirable for her to try to distance herself from her respondents, who, together with her, would become equal contributors to the findings. The effect of the researcher's presence, style and contributions can therefore be addressed in the discussion of the findings, producing an account which is much more reflexive (that is, it comments upon its own method of production) than would be possible within the traditional framework.

However, there is a further difficulty to be addressed concerning the status of individuals' accounts of themselves. Psychologists who have been influenced by poststructuralist theories (see Chapter 5) often argue that we should not take people's accounts at face value. Whereas within the experimental paradigm such accounts are devalued because they are not measurable observations of behaviour, within a poststructuralist framework they become problematic because it is argued that our thoughts and feelings are not simply properties of our own individual psyches but are social productions, having their roots in the social structures and practices that form the fabric of our daily lives. Within this view, the narratives we weave around our experience are not of our own personal making, but are representations we come to adopt because they are the ways that people in our particular society tend to make sense of their experience; and these particular ways of sense-making are intimately tied to social structures and power relations. For example, Kitzinger (1987, 1989) describes how, in her interviews with lesbian women, they often told a story of their sexual relationships using themes of romantic love, family life and personal liberty. However, she argues that these ways of accounting are the products of our particular social arrangements, where the heterosexual family, married life and the subordination of women are necessary to the status quo. Thus the lesbian women she interviewed were experiencing their lives and accounting for them in ways which are derived from an inegalitarian social structure and which, in the end, are probably not in the long term political interests of themselves and other lesbians.

There has therefore been a rising interest in methods which do not take accounts at face value, such as discourse analysis. While interviews are very often the material upon which this is performed, the aim of the analysis is not to reveal what the person truly thinks or feels (which, within this theoretical perspective, becomes a very problematic idea in itself) but to identify the discourses, representations and ideologies which are flowing through a person's talk in order to theorise how our representations of ourselves are linked to inequalities and power relations (see Burr, 1995 for a brief account of discourse analysis).

The methods of depth interviewing and discourse analysis, and the theoretical analysis behind them, are obviously not just relevant to gender and are of value in a variety of areas. Nevertheless, it seems to be the case that they have been taken up enthusiastically by feminist researchers in particular.

### Who can do feminist research?

In theory, it would seem to be possible for men as well as women to carry out research which has a feminist agenda, just as it is theoretically possible for men to be feminists. Nevertheless, it is sometimes argued that only women can effectively perform feminist research, since common experience and a common social position are necessary to bring about the sense of connectedness and empathy which is the core of the approach. Although this argument has some validity, it must be pointed out that women, like men, are divided by class, education, ethnicity, religion and so on which may be at least as powerful as gender, so that for example middle class women may have more in common with middle class men than they do with working class women.

Finally, there is a more radical question about whether the tenets of feminist research are in any way compatible with any form of psychology that psychologists would recognise. Although the aim of providing more opportunities for women psychologists to do research and to publish their work seems a worthwhile one, simply adding more women into the discipline in this way does not necessarily solve the problems that have been identified with the practice of psychology itself. Female psychology under-graduates are educated in the assumptions and practices of traditional psychology just as much as their male counterparts, and it would be folly to assume that encouraging more women researchers would automatically bring about a change in ethos in the discipline. However, many women psychologists doubt the possibility of carrying out research which is both feminist and psychological. Burman (1990) argues that the inherent individu-alism of psychology (the idea that the individual and its social context are separable and that the person can be meaningfully studied in isolation) is absolutely counter to a feminist approach to research. Other feminists take a less pessimistic stance and have attempted to bring their practice and teaching of psychology in line with feminist principles (see Squire, 1990b; Wilkinson, 1986).

## Summary

In this chapter I have examined some of the most common ways in which psychologists have studied gender in the past. Sex differ-ences research and studies using measures of masculinity and femininity (or masculinity–femininity) have enjoyed great popu-larity with psychologists. However, this research has been criticised for its reliance upon sexist assumptions. Although efforts to reconceptualise masculinity and femininity are praiseworthy, for example through the concept of androgyny and gender schema theory, they too rest ultimately on assumptions that locate gender as an intra-psychic phenomenon disconnected from wider social conditions. However, the problem is not limited to psychological research on gender, but seems to implicate psychology as a deeply inequitous discipline itself. The methods and assumptions of psychology, in particular its claim to be objective, value-free and apolitical, have been challenged by some feminists who have recommended a more democratic research process with an emphasis upon qualitative methods. While some feminists have promoted such a move within psychology, others doubt that the fundamental assumptions of psychology and feminism are ultimately compatible.

## Further reading

Bem, S.L. (1993) *The Lenses of Gender: Transforming the Debate on Sexual Inequality*, New Haven: Yale University Press. An engaging book, drawing on examples from everyday life to illustrate the gender 'lenses' through which we view the world.

Henriques, J., Hollway, W., Urwin, C., Venn, C. and Walkerdine, V. (1984) *Changing the Subject: Psychology, Social Regulation and Subjectivity*, London and New York: Methuen. This collection of chapters examines the way that psychology constructs us as its 'subjects'. The areas of work, racism, child psychology, gender and power relations are covered, and it includes a chapter on the construction of the 'subject' in psychology. The chapters do vary in their accessibility, however.

Wilkinson, S. (ed.) (1986) *Feminist Social Psychology*, Milton Keynes: Open University Press. Now a classic collection of chapters showing how feminism might transform the practice of social psychology.

# Glossary

The first occurrence of each of these terms is highlighted in **bold** type in the main text.

**behaviourism** School of psychological theory which holds that the observation and description of overt behaviour are all that is needed to understand human beings.

**determinism** A style of thinking in which all human action or experience is assumed to be directly caused.

**discourse** A systematic, coherent set of images, metaphors and ways of talking that constructs or represents an object in a particular way.

**domestic gender division of labour** The division of household and childcare tasks between women and men in the home.

**equity theory** The idea that, in our social encounters, we compare our own outcomes with those of our partners and try to ensure that the payoffs for each of us is 'fair' in terms of the effort we have put in.

**essentialism** The view that objects (including people) have an essential, inherent nature which can be discovered. The idea that human beings have an 'essence' or fixed nature that is expressed in their behaviour.

**exchange theory** The idea that people try to maximise their gains and minimise their costs in a relationship, and that partners will reciprocate (exchange) the rewards they receive from their partner.

**experiment** Observation of a behaviour or phenomenon under conditions that are controlled by the experimenter.

**femininity** The social and cultural expectations, in terms of behaviours and traits, attached to being a woman.

**feminism** A social movement aiming to benefit women. Theories and forms of action aimed at eradicating gender (and sometimes other) inequalities.

**gender** The social significance of sex.

**gender role (or sex role)** The set of behaviours, duties and expectations attached to the status of being a man or a woman.

**horizontal gender division of labour** The division in paid work whereby there are jobs that are performed mainly by women and jobs that are performed mainly by men.

**learning theory** 'Learning' broadly refers to the acquisition and storage of information by an animal in a way that allows it to modify its behaviour in the future. However, the term 'learning theory' is often used specifically to refer to psychological theories which describe the rules and principles by which behaviour is acquired.

**masculinity** The social and cultural expectations, in terms of behaviours and traits, attached to being a man.

**modelling** Learning by imitation, by copying a 'model'.

**paid work** This term is used (rather than simply 'work') to refer to work performed for an income in order to highlight the fact that 'housework' is also 'work' but is not paid. This is a point particularly emphasised by Marxist feminists.

**patriarchy** A society or system of social structures dominated by men.

**psychoanalysis** Branch of psychology and therapeutic approach, originated by Sigmund Freud. It focuses upon the role of early experience and unconscious emotions and motivations in producing our behaviour, especially maladaptive or neurotic behaviour.

**psychometrics** Branch of psychology concerned with mental testing of many kinds.

**qualitative methods**   Research methods, such as depth interviewing, where the data gathered are semantic (they are in the form of 'meanings' or descriptions) rather than numerical (quantitative data).

**reductionism**   Style of thinking or theory which reduces complex phenomena to simpler, component parts.

**reinforcement**   The strengthening or encouragement of a behavioural response by giving a reward or by the removal of an unpleasant stimulus.

**role**   A central concept in social psychology, which refers to the behaviour expected of a person in accordance with the position they hold in their society.

**sex discrimination**   Treating people less favourably on the basis of their sex.

**sexual harassment**   There are various definitions of this, but they usually include unwanted sexual advances by a man toward a woman (although theoretically men can also be victims of sexual harassment).

**social constructionism**   The view that people are not determined by biological or environmental influences, but that they are 'constructed' through the processes of interpersonal interaction and through language.

**social learning theory**   This theory argues that we acquire various behaviours by observation or imitation. *See also* **vicarious reinforcement**.

**socialisation**   The processes by which an individual comes to adopt the norms of appropriate behaviour in their society.

**sociobiology**   The study of possible genetic bases of social behaviour and societal phenomena.

**stereotype**   An over simplified, prejudicial belief which tends to persist despite evidence to the contrary.

**vertical gender division of labour**   The division in the labour market whereby men generally hold higher status and better paid jobs than women, even within the same kind of occupation.

**vicarious reinforcement**   This is where a behaviour is learned through watching another person being rewarded for similar behaviours.

# References

Abraham, J. (1995) *Divide and School: Gender and Class Dynamics in Comprehensive Education*, London: Falmer Press.

Acker, S. (1994) *Gendered Education*, Buckingham: Open University Press.

Anderson, R. (1988) *The Power and the Word: Language, Power and Change*, London: Paladin.

Antill, J.K. and Cotton, S. (1988) 'Factors affecting the division of labour in households', *Sex Roles*, 18, 9/10: 531–53.

Archer, J. (1992) 'Sex bias in evaluations at college and work', *The Psychologist*, 5, 200–204.

Archer, J. and Lloyd, B.B. (1981) 'Problems and issues in research on gender differences', *Current Psychological Reviews*, 1: 287–304.

Archer, J. and Lloyd, B.B. (1985) *Sex and Gender*, Cambridge: Cambridge University Press.

Armistead, N. (1974) *Reconstructing Social Psychology*, Harmondsworth: Penguin.

Arnot, M. and Weiner, G. (1987) *Gender and the Politics of Schooling*, London: Hutchinson.

Askew, S. and Ross, C. (1988) *Boys Don't Cry: Boys and Sexism in Education*, Buckingham: Open University Press.

Backett, K. (1987) 'The negotiation of fatherhood', in C. Lewis and M. O'Brien, (eds) *Reassessing Fatherhood*, London: Sage.

Ballaster, R., Beetham, M., Frazer. E. and Hebron, S. (1991) *Women's Worlds: Ideology, Femininity and the Woman's Magazine*, Basingstoke: Macmillan.

Barrett, M. (1988) *Women's Oppression Today: The Marxist/Feminist Encounter*, London: Verso.

Beloff, H. (1992) 'Mother, father and me: our IQ', *The Psychologist*, July, 309–11.

Bem, S.L. (1974) 'The measurement of psychological androgyny', *Journal of Consulting and Clinical Psychology*, 42: 155–62.

Bem, S.L. (1981) 'Gender schema theory: A cognitive assessment of sex-typing', *Psychological Review*, 88, 354–64.

Bem, S.L. (1993) *The Lenses of Gender: Transforming the Debate on Sexual Inequality*, New Haven: Yale University Press.

Berger, J. (1972) *Ways of Seeing*, London: Penguin.

Boulton, M.G. (1983) *On Being a Mother*, London: Tavistock.

Bowlby, J. (1952) *Maternal Care and Mental Health*, World Health Organisation, Geneva (first published 1951).

Brittan, A. and Maynard, M. (1984) *Sexism, Racism and Oppression*, Oxford: Blackwell.

Broverman, I.K., Broverman, D.M., Clarkson, H., Rosenkrantz, P. and Vogel, S. (1970) 'Sex-role stereotypes and clinical judgements of mental health', *Journal of Consulting and Clinical Psychology*, 34, 1: 1–7.

Brown, P. (1973) *Radical Psychology*, London: Tavistock.

Brownmiller, S. (1975) *Against Our Will: Men, Women and Rape*, London: Secker and Warburg.

Bryson, V. (1992) *Feminist Political Theory: An Introduction*, Basingstoke: Macmillan.

Buckingham, D. (1993) 'Boys' talk: television and the policing of masculinity', in D. Buckingham (ed.) *Reading Audiences: Young People and the Media*, Manchester: Manchester University Press.

Burman, E. (ed.) (1990) *Feminists and Psychological Practice*, London: Sage.

Burr, V. (1995) *An Introduction to Social Constructionism*, London: Routledge.

Cameron, D. (1992) *Feminism and Linguistic Theory* (second edition), Basingstoke: Macmillan.

Cameron, D. (1995) *Verbal Hygiene*, London: Routledge.

Chodorow, N. (1978) *The Reproduction of Mothering*, Berkeley: University of California Press.

Clarricoates, K. (1978) 'Dinosaurs in the classroom: A re-examination of some aspects of the "hidden curriculum" in primary schools', *Women's Studies International Quarterly*, 1: 353–64.

Clarricoates, K. (1980) 'The importance of being Ernest . . . Tom . . . Jane: The perception and categorization of gender conformity and gender deviation in primary schools', In R. Deem (ed.) *Schooling for Women's Work*, London: Routledge and Kegan Paul.

Constantinople, A. (1973) 'Masculinity–Femininity: An exception to a famous dictum?' *Psychological Bulletin*, 80, 5: 389–407.

Courtney, A.E. and Whipple, T.W. (1983) *Sex Stereotyping in Advertising*, Lexington, Mass.: Lexington Books.

Croghan, R. (1991) 'First time mothers' accounts of inequality in the division of labour', *Feminism and Psychology*, 1, 2: 221–46.

Daly, M. (1979) *Gyn/Ecology: The Metaethics of Radical Feminism*, London: The Women's Press.

Daly, M. (1984) *Pure Lust: Elemental Feminist Philosophy*, London: The Women's Press.

Davies, B. and Harré, R. (1990) 'Positioning: the discursive production of selves', *Journal for the Theory of Social Behaviour*, 20, 1: 43–63.

Deem, R. (ed.) (1984) *Coeducation Reconsidered*, Milton Keynes: Open University Press.

Delphy, C. (1980) 'A materialist feminism is possible', *Feminist Review*, 4.

Department For Education (DFE) (1993) *Statistical Bulletin*, 26: December.

Durkin, K. (1985) *Television, Sex Roles and Children: A Developmental Social Psychological Account*, Milton Keynes: Open University Press.

Dworkin, A. (1981) *Pornography: Men Possessing Women*, London: The Women's Press.

Eagly, A. (1983) 'Gender and social influence: a social psychological analysis', *American Psychologist*, September.

Easthope, A. (1986) *What a Man's Gotta Do: The Masculine Myth in Popular Culture*, London: Paladin.

Edley, N. and Wetherell, M. (1995) *Men in Perspective: Practice, Power and Identity*, Hemel Hempstead: Prentice Hall/Harvester Wheatsheaf.

Eisenstein, H. (1984) *Contemporary Feminist Thought*, London: Unwin.

EOC (1996) *Facts about Women and Men in Great Britain*, Manchester: EOC.

Epstein, D. (1993) *Changing Classroom Cultures: Anti-racism, Politics and Schools*, Stoke-on-Trent: Trentham Books Ltd.

Fausto-Sterling, A. (1985) *Myths of Gender: Biological Theories about Men and Women*, New York: Basic Books.

Ferguson, M. (1983) *Forever Feminine: Women's Magazines and the Cult of Femininity*, London: Heinemann.

Firestone, S. (1971) *The Dialectic of Sex*, London: Cape.

Firth-Cozens, J. and West. M. (eds) (1990) *Women at Work: Psychological and Organizational Perspectives*, Buckingham: Open University Press.

Foucault, M. (1972) *The Archaeology of Knowledge*, London: Tavistock.

French, J. (1985) 'Gender and the classroom', *New Society*, March.

French, J. and French, P. (1993) 'Gender imbalances in the primary classroom', in P. Woods and M. Hammersley (eds) *Gender and Ethnicity in Schools: Ethnographic Accounts*, Buckingham: Open University Press.

Fromm, M. (1967) 'Psychoanalytic considerations on abortion', in H. Rosen (ed.) *Abortion in America*, Boston: Beacon.

Frosh, S. (1987) *The Politics of Psychoanalysis: An Introduction to Freudian and Post-Freudian Theory*, London: Macmillan.

Furnham, A. and Schofield, S. (1986) 'Sex-role stereotyping in British radio advertisements', *British Journal of Social Psychology*, 25, 2: 165–71.

Giddens, A. (1989) *Sociology*, Cambridge: Polity Press.

Gilligan, C. (1977) 'In a different voice: women's conceptions of self and of morality', *Harvard Educational Review*, 47, 4: 481–517.

Gilligan, C. (1982) *In a Different Voice*, Cambridge, Mass.: Harvard University Press.

Goffman, E. (1961) *Encounters*, London: Allen Lane The Penguin Press.

Goffman, E. (1976) *Gender Advertisements*, New York and London: Harper and Row.

Grafton, T., Miller, H., Smith, L., Vegoda, M. and Whitfield, R. (1987) 'Gender and curriculum choice', in M. Arnot and G. Weiner (eds) *Gender and the Politics of Schooling*, London: Hutchinson Education.

Gunter, B. (1986) *Television and Sex-Role Stereotyping*, London: John Libbey.

Harding, S. (1991) *Whose Science? Whose Knowledge?: Thinking from Women's Lives*, Buckingham: Open University Press.

Hardy, M.T. (1989) 'Girls, science and gender bias in instructional materials', *Occasional Papers on Aspects of Primary Education*, Nottingham School of Education, University of Nottingham.

Hargreaves, D.J. and Colley, A.M. (eds) (1986) *The Psychology of Sex Roles*, London: Harper Row.

Henriques, J., Hollway, W., Urwin, C., Venn, C. and Walkerdine, V. (1984) *Changing the Subject: Psychology, Social Regulation and Subjectivity*, London and New York: Methuen.

Hollway, W. (1989) *Subjectivity and Method in Psychology: Gender, Meaning and Science*, London: Sage.

Hood, J. (ed.) (1993) *Men, Work and Family*, Newbury Park, Calif.: Sage.

Horna, J. and Lupri, E. (1987) 'Fathers' participation in work, family life and leisure: a Canadian experience', in C. Lewis and M. O'Brien (eds) *Reassessing Fatherhood*, London: Sage.

Howitt, D. (1991) *Concerning Psychology: Psychology Applied to Social Issues*, Buckingham: Open University Press.

Jones, C. and Mahoney, P. (1989) *Learning Our Lines: Sexuality and Social Control in Education*, London: The Women's Press.

Kagan, C. and Lewis, S. (1990) '"Where's your sense of humour?" Swimming against the tide in higher education', in E. Burman (ed.) *Feminists and Psychological Practice*, London: Sage.

Kelly, A. (1985) 'The construction of masculine science', *British Journal of Sociology of Education*, 6: 133–54.

Kelly, G.A. (1955) *The Psychology of Personal Constructs*, New York: Norton.

Kimmel, D.C. (1980) *Adulthood and Aging: An Interdisciplinary, Developmental View* (second edition), New York: John Wiley and Sons.

Kitzinger, C. (1987) *The Social Construction of Lesbianism*, London: Sage.

Kitzinger, C. (1989) 'The regulation of lesbian identities: liberal humanism as an ideology of social control', in J. Shotter and K.J. Gergen (eds) *Texts of Identity*, London: Sage.

Kitzinger, C. (1992) 'The individuated self-concept: a critical analysis of social constructionist writing on individualism', in G. Breakwell (ed.) *Social Psychology of Identity and the Self Concept*, London: Surrey University Press in association with Academic Press.

Kling, A. (1975) 'Testosterone and aggressive behaviour in men and non-human primates', in B. Eleftheriori and R. Spot (eds) *Hormonal Correlates of Behaviour*, New York: Plenum.

Kohlberg, L. (1964) 'Development of moral character and moral ideology', in M.L. Hoffman and L.W. Hoffman (eds) *Review of Child Development Research*, 1, New York: Russel Sage Foundation.

Kohlberg, L. (1966) 'A cognitive developmental analysis of children's sex role concepts and attitudes', in E.E. Maccoby (ed.) *The Development of Sex Differences*, Stanford, Calif.: Stanford University Press.

Kohlberg, L. (1969) 'Stage and sequence: the cognitive–developmental approach to socialization', in D.A. Goslin (ed.) *Handbook of Socialization Theory and Research*, Chicago: Rand McNally.

Kohlberg, L. (1981) *The Philosophy of Moral Development*, New York: Harper Row.

Kohlberg, L. and Kramer, R. (1967) 'Continuities and discontinuities in childhood and adult moral development', *Human Development*, 12: 93–120.

Kreuz, L.E. and Rose, R.M. (1972) 'Assessment of aggressive behaviour and plasma testosterone in a young criminal population', *Psychosomatic Medicine*, 34.

Levinson, D.J., Darrow, C.N., Klein, E.B., Levinson, M.H. and McKee, B. (1978) *The Seasons of a Man's Life*, New York: Knopf.

Lewis, C. (1986) *Becoming a Father*, Milton Keynes: Open University Press.

Lewis, C. and O'Brien, M. (1987) *Reassessing Fatherhood*, London: Sage.

Lobban, G. (1975) 'Sex roles in reading schemes', *Educational Review*, 27: 202–10.

Mac an Ghaill, M. (1994) *The Making of Men: Masculinities, Sexualities and Schooling*, Buckingham: Open University Press.

Maccoby, E. and Jacklin, C.N. (1974) *The Psychology of Sex Differences*, London: Oxford University Press.

MacKinnon, C. (1989) 'Sexuality, pornography and method: pleasure under patriarchy', *Ethics*, 99, 2.

McRobbie, A. (1982) 'Jackie: an ideology of adolescent femininity', in B. Waites, T. Bennett and G. Martin (eds) *Popular Culture, Past and Present*, London: Croom Helm and the Open University Press.

McRobbie, A. (1991) *Feminism and Youth Culture: From 'Jackie' to 'Just Seventeen'*, Basingstoke: Macmillan Education.

Mahoney, P. (1985) *Schools for the Boys? Co-education Reassessed*, London: Hutchinson.

Malinowski, B. (1932) *The Sexual Lives of Savages*, New York: Routledge.

Marshall, H. and Wetherell, M. (1989) 'Talking about career and gender identities: a discourse analysis perspective', in S. Skevington and D. Baker (eds) *The Social Identity of Women*, London: Sage.

Mead, M. (1935) *Sex and Temperament*, New York: William Morrow and Mentor.

Meyer-Bahlberg, H.F.L. *et al.* (1974) 'Aggressiveness and testosterone measures in man', *Psychosomatic Medicine*, 36: 267–74.

Miles, S. and Middleton, C. (1990) 'Girls' education in the balance', in M. Flude and M. Hammer (eds) *The Education Reform Act 1988*, London: Falmer Press.

Miller, Jean Baker (1976) *Toward a New Psychology of Women*, Boston: Beacon Press.

Mintel (1993) *Women 2000*, London: Mintel International Group.

Mischel, W. (1966) 'A social learning view of sex differences in behaviour', in E.E. Maccoby (ed.) *The Development of Sex Differences*, Stanford, Calif.: Stanford University Press.

Modleski, T. (1984) *Loving with a Vengeance: Mass Produced Fantasies for Women*, New York and London: Methuen.

Moir, A. and Jessel, D. (1989) *Brain Sex: The Real Difference between Men and Women*, London: Michael Joseph.

Money, J. and Ehrhardt, A.A. (1972) *Man and Woman, Boy and Girl*, Baltimore: Johns Hopkins University Press.

Moss, G. (1993) 'Girls tell the teen romance', in D. Buckingham (ed.) *Reading Audiences: Young People and the Media*, Manchester: Manchester University Press.

Moss, H.A. (1967) 'Sex, age and state as determinants of mother–infant interaction', *Merrill–Palmer Quarterly*, 13, 19–36.

Nardi, P.M. (ed.) (1992) *Men's Friendships*, London: Sage.

Newson, J., Newson, E., Richardson, D. and Scaife, J. (1978) 'Perspectives in sex role stereotyping', in Chetwynd, J. and Hartnett, O. (eds) *The Sex Role System: Psychological and Sociological Perspectives*, London: Routledge and Kegan Paul.

Oakley, A. (1974) *The Sociology of Housework*, Oxford: Martin Robertson.

Oakley, A. (1981a) *Subject Women*, London: Fontana.

Oakley, A. (1981b) 'Interviewing women: A contradiction in terms', in H. Roberts (ed.) *Doing Feminist Research*, London: Routledge.

Parke, R.D. (1967) 'Nurturance, nurturance withdrawal and resistance to deviation', *Child Development*, 38: 1101–10.

Parsons, T. and Bales, R.F. (1953) Family, Socialisation and Interaction Process, Glencoe, Ill.: Free Press.

Persky, H. Smith, K.D. and Basu, G.K. (1971) 'Relations of psychological measures of aggression and hostility to testosterone production in man', *Psychosomatic Medicine*, 33: 265–77.

Piercy, M. (1978) *Woman on the Edge of Time*, London: The Women's Press.

Pleck, J.H. (1979) 'Men's family work: three perspectives and some new data', *The Family Coordinator*, October.

Pleck, J.H. (1993) 'Are "family-supportive" employer policies relevant to men?', in J.C. Hood (ed.) *Men, Work and Family*, Newbury Park, Calif.: Sage.

*Polity Reader in Gender Studies* (1994), Cambridge: Polity Press.

Pratt, J. (1985) 'The attitudes of teachers', in J. Whyte, R. Deem, L. Kant and M. Cruickshank (eds) *Girl Friendly Schooling*, London: Methuen.

Raymond, J. (1979) *The Transsexual Empire: The Making of the She-Male*, Boston: Beacon Press.

Rogers, D. (1986) *The Adult Years: An Introduction to Aging* (third edition), Englewood Cliffs, N.J.: Prentice-Hall.

Root, J. (1984) *Pictures of Women*, London: Pandora.

Rose, R.M. (1975) 'Testosterone, aggression and homosexuality: a review of the literature and implications for future research', in E.J. Sachar (ed.) *Topics in Psychoendocrinology*, New York: Grune and Stratton.

Rose, S., Lewontin, R.C. and Kamin, L.J. (1990) *Not in our Genes: Biology, Ideology and Human Nature*, Harmondsworth: Penguin.

Rosenthal, R. and Jacobson, L. (1968) *Pygmalion in the Classroom*, New York: Holt, Rinehart and Winston.

Ruddock, J. (1994) *Developing a Gender Policy in Secondary Schools*, Buckingham: Open University Press.

Russel, G. (1983) *The Changing Role of Fathers?*, St Lucia, Queensland: University of Queensland Press.

Salmon, P. (1995) *Psychology in the Classroom: Reconstructing Teachers and Learners*, London: Cassell.

Sampson, E.E. (1990) 'Social psychology and social control', in I. Parker and J. Shotter (eds) *Deconstructing Social Psychology*, London: Routledge.

Sayers J. (1982) *Biological Politics: Feminist and Anti-feminist Perspectives*, London: Tavistock.

Scanzoni, J. (1970) *Opportunity and the Family*, New York: Free Press.

Scott, M. (1988) 'Patriarchy in school textbooks', in R. Dale, R. Fergusson and A. Robinson (eds) *Frameworks for Teaching: Readings for the Intending Secondary Teacher*, London: Hodder and Stoughton in association with the Open University.

Segal, L. (1990) *Slow Motion: Changing Masculinities, Changing Men*: New Brunswick, N.J.: Rutgers University Press.

Sherif, C.W. (1987) 'Bias in psychology', in S. Harding (ed.) *Feminism and Methodology*, Milton Keynes: Open University Press.

Shotter, J. (1990) 'Social individuality versus possessive individualism: the sounds of silence', in I. Parker and J. Shotter (eds) *Deconstructing Social Psychology*, London: Routledge.

Spear, M.G. (1985) 'Teachers' attitudes towards girls and technology', in J. Whyte. R. Deem, L. Kant and M. Cruickshank (eds) *Girl-Friendly Schooling*, London: Methuen.

Spender, D. (1980) *Man Made Language*, London: Routledge.

Spender, D. (1981) 'The gatekeepers: a feminist critique of academic publishing', in H. Roberts (ed.) *Doing Feminist Research*, London: Routledge.

Spender, D. (1982) *Invisible Women*, London: The Women's Press.

Squire, C. (1989) *Significant Differences: Feminism in Psychology*, London: Routledge.

Squire, C. (1990a) 'Crisis what crisis? Discourses and narratives of the "social" in social psychology', in I. Parker and J. Shotter (eds) *Deconstructing Social Psychology*, London: Routledge.

Squire, C. (1990b) 'Feminism as antipsychology: learning and teaching in feminist psychology', in E. Burman (ed.) *Feminists and Psychological Practice*, London: Sage.

Stanworth, M. (1983) *Gender and Schooling: A Study of Sexual Division in the Classroom*, London: Hutchinson.

Star, S.L. (1991) 'The politics of left and right: sex differences in hemispheric brain asymmetry', in S. Gunew (ed.) *A Reader in Feminist Knowledge*, London: Routledge.

Stouwie, R.J. (1971) 'Inconsistent verbal instructions and children's resistance to temptation behaviour', *Child Development*, 42: 1517–31.

Strong, E.K. (1936) 'Interests of men and women', *Journal of Social Psychology*, 13: 49–67.

Swann, J. (1992) *Girls, Boys and Language*, Oxford: Blackwell.

Tempest, E. (1990) *Telling It Like It Is ...* , Unpublished paper, University of Bradford.

Tennan, L. and Miles, C.C. (1936) *Sex and Personality*, New York: McGraw-Hill.

Thorne, B. (1993) *Gender Play: Girls and Boys in Schools*, Buckingham: Open University Press.

Tong, R. (1989) *Feminist Thought: A Comprehensive Introduction*, London: Routledge.

Trowler, P. (1995) *Investigating Education and Training*, London: Harper Collins.

Ussher, J. (1989) *The Psychology of the Female Body*, London: Routledge.

Ussher, J. (1990) 'Choosing psychology or not throwing the baby out with the bathwater', in E. Burman (ed.) *Feminists and Psychological Practice*, London: Sage.

Walby, S. (1990) *Theorizing Patriarchy*, Oxford: Blackwell.

Walkerdine, V. (1987) 'No laughing matter: girls' comics and the preparation for adolescent sexuality', in J.M. Broughton (ed.) *Critical Theories of Psychological Development*, New York: Plenum Press.

Walkerdine, V. (1993) 'Femininity as performance', in L. Stone (ed.) *The Education Feminism Reader*, London: Routledge.

Walkerdine, V. and Melody, J. (1993) ' "Daddy's gonna buy you a dream to cling to (and mummy's gonna love you just as much as she can)": young girls and popular television', in D. Buckingham (ed.) *Reading Audiences: Young People and the Media*, Manchester: Manchester University Press.

Walum, L.R. (1977) *The Dynamics of Sex and Gender: A Sociological Perspective*, Chicago: Rand McNally.

Watson, J.B. (1930) *Behaviourism*, Chicago, Ill.: University of Chicago Press.

Weedon, C. (1987) *Feminist Practice and Poststructuralist Theory*, Oxford: Blackwell.

Weiner, G. (1994) *Feminisms in Education: An Introduction*, Buckingham: Open University Press.

White, A. (1989) *Poles Apart? The Experience of Gender*, London: J.M. Dent and Sons Ltd.

Wilkinson, S. (ed.)(1986) *Feminist Social Psychology*, Buckingham: Open University Press.

Will, J.A., Self, P.A. and Datan, N. (1976) 'Maternal behaviour and perceived sex of infant', *American Journal of Orthopsychiatry*, 46: 135–39.

Willis, P. (1977) *Learning to Labour: How Working Class Kids get Working Class Jobs*, Farnborough: Saxon House.

Wilson, E.O. (1975) 'Human decency is animal', *New York Times Magazine*, October 12: 38–50.

Woods, P. (1990) *Teacher Skills and Strategies*, Lewes: Falmer.

# Index